How to Turn Procrastination into Productivity

A Successful Man's Guide to the Psychology of Self-Discipline, Time Management, and Motivation + 20 Powerful Daily Habits to Achieve Success and Mastery

Written by David Bailey

How to Turn Procrastination into Productivity

© Copyright 2018 by David Bailey - All rights reserved.

The following eBook is reproduced below with the goal of providing information that is as accurate and reliable as possible. Regardless, purchasing this eBook can be seen as consent to the fact that both the publisher and the author of this book are in no way experts on the topics discussed within and that any recommendations or suggestions that are made herein are for entertainment purposes only. Professionals should be consulted as needed prior to undertaking any of the action endorsed herein.

This declaration is deemed fair and valid by both the American Bar Association and the Committee of Publishers Association and is legally binding throughout the United States.

Furthermore, the transmission, duplication or reproduction of any of the following work including specific information will be considered an illegal act irrespective of if it is done electronically or in print. This extends to creating a secondary or tertiary copy of the work or a recorded copy and is only allowed with an expressed written consent from the Publisher. All additional rights reserved.

The information in the following pages is broadly considered to be a truthful and accurate account of facts and as such any inattention, use or misuse of the information in question by the reader will render any resulting actions solely under their purview. There are no scenarios in which the publisher or the original author of this work can be in any fashion deemed liable for any hardship or damages that may befall them after undertaking information described herein.

Additionally, the information in the following pages is intended only for informational purposes and should thus be thought of as universal. As befitting its nature, it is presented without assurance regarding its prolonged validity or interim quality. Trademarks that are mentioned are done without written consent and can in no way be considered an endorsement from the trademark holder.

David Bailey
Table of Contents

Introduction 6

Chapter One: Powerful Goal Setting Secrets 22

Chapter Two: Internalize Your Goals 51

Chapter Three: Tackling the Procrastination Monster Head On 87

Chapter Four: Time Management Secrets 115

Chapter Five: Be the Ultimate Self-Discipline Ninja 135

Conclusion 161

Introduction

"Self-discipline begins with the mastery of your thoughts. If you don't control what you think, you can't control what you do. Simply, self-discipline enables you to think first and act afterward." – Napoleon Hill

There was once a great king who had heard about a master sword crafter who was said to be on par with Picasso when it came to his genius. The king decided he must meet this master sword crafter at once. He summoned his guards to find the sword crafter and bring him to the palace. The king's guards ran in all directions, looking for the maestro sword crafter, and finally found him in a tiny village on the outskirts of the kingdom. As ordered, they brought him before the king.

The master walked him humbly, graciously and gently, and the king responded similarly. The king then posed him a question he would ask all maestros. "Oh, sword crafter, what is true secret to your extraordinariness or excellence in what you do?" Pat came the reply from the sword crafter, "ever since I was a child, I became exposed to the art of making swords and fell madly in love with it. It seldom spoke to my brain, head or logic. Instead it spoke to me at a much deeper level and soulful level. It tugged at my heart. As a child, I decided that I will be a master at sword crafting. Growing up, I read plenty of books about sword crafting. If a thing didn't relate to sword crafting, didn't have the word sword in it, didn't look like a sword or had nothing to do with sword crafting, I wouldn't spend my time on it. That is the true secret of my mastery.

Let this powerful parable sink in your head for a while because, in many ways, this is the secret to being exceptional, extraordinary, world class! We function in a world inundated with distractions and fruitless pursuits. We are constantly pulled in different directions, and operate on auto-pilot, mindlessly going about things. This makes us time and productivity starved! Focus on few things that are important

Let begin with a small and exciting exercise. What are the five most important things in your life? Maybe career/business, family, personal development, art, travel – whatever. Just pick five things that are most important and hold maximum value/relevance in your life. Now passionately build your life around it. Focus your time, energy efforts and much more on these all-important five things.

Clear all the other clutter and noise surrounding you that doesn't relate to or align with these five swords. This is, in essence, the secret to being productive. There are plenty of people who get bored and spend their most productive hours playing aggressive games, browsing through Instagram and checking their Facebook for the nth time.

They'll convince you they are being productive because they always look preoccupied. Looking busy doesn't necessarily mean they are being productive. What are you busy doing is the key? Are you doing something that is adding value to your overall goals? Are you busy doing things that are in alignment with your five swords? People won't distance themselves from what they are doing or step back and take an objective look at whether they are indeed involved in productive acts that are in alignment with their overall goals. They are in effect giving their best hours of their best days to nothing more than shiny objects.

Each time you find yourself digressing from your goals, think of the sword crafters metaphor. Dedicate yourself to the five things that matter most in your life (and let one of those five things not be Netflix or PlayStation). Be among the 1 percent that focuses on things which really matter. Pull the courage to say no to activities and people who call for your time to make you unproductive. Have the fortitude to say no to activities that appear desirable or shiny but are plain hollow or have no value. This is the pathway to success, wealth and life mastery. True leaders aren't just ones with fancy titles.

True leaders are those who inspire others with their work, self-discipline, and productivity.

Let's do another interesting and enjoyable exercise. Ready? Grab a notepad and paper and write down the names of 10 people on this planet you admire the most. Yes, 10 people whose life really admire, and seek inspiration from! It can be your favorite sports star, an entrepreneur, a technical wizard, an inventor, a movie star – just about anyone you truly, deeply admire. Take your time and think hard.

Done writing? Now, look for a common trait in all these people (other than the fact that they are all your idols of course). What is that one single trait which makes them all admirably successful? My bets are on self-discipline!

There is no long-term success with self-discipline, which drives a person's ability to be productive and action-oriented. The people you admire is all hustlers. They keep getting things done, explore newer horizons, and follow effective habits to reach their goals. Self-discipline distinguishes the average from the extraordinary.

Notice how there is always a split-second difference between athletes in crucial races. However, despite winning by a split-second margin, the winner takes it all, while the athlete in second place has to contend with much lesser rewards. Though the difference was only in split seconds, the awards for winners are much greater. This split-second difference is self-discipline. The ability to get yourself to do things! The ability to be productive and hustle your way to success, money, and mastery! The ability to go from ordinary to exceptional!

Unfortunately, there's no magic wand or potion for success and mastery. Much as I'd love you to be successful immediately, it's a gradual process. Attaining success is more like cooking in a crockpot than microwave. The microwave mentality of quick success and quicker failure doesn't last. Success has to brew for long if you want its flavor to sustain. You don't just have to adopt a successful mindset but also habits of successful masters who stand as testimony for the fact that building wealth, success and life mastery need a conscious cultivation of self-discipline and powerful success habits. Are you geared for success? Much of it will be determined by tracking your daily habits and self-discipline patterns?

I remember having an interesting conversation with a friend once, where he mentioned that a majority of successful people just happen to be at the right place at the right time. They get plain lucky. Yes, I'd say being lucky can get you that one shot at success. However, without self-discipline and these 20 powerful habits that I am going to discuss, the success won't last.

Successful people display amazing time management skills, accept accountability for their actions, operate with a solution-oriented mindset, and have the tenacity to transform challenges into opportunities. They demonstrate great restrain self-control, and the ability to delay greater while firmly fixating their eyes on the bigger picture or goals.

People with a success, wealth and mastery mindset almost always have their actions driven by keeping their eyes firmly on long-term rewards. This is the one trait that separates winners from strugglers. They are able to delay gratification or give up short-term pleasures in exchange for long-term rewards. Whether you are going to be a struggler or winner is in your hands? You alone are responsible for the choices you make!

There is no denying the element of luck and good fortune in writing a person's success. However, this success is also a direct result of meticulously cultivated and nurtured habits, actions, mindset, beliefs, and thoughts. We are nothing but an aggregation of our habits, thoughts, beliefs, and actions. Self-discipline and success habits (I like to call them success habits) are the ultimate bridge to achieving your goals.

Were you aware that 40 percent of all our behavior is determined by habits? If you are wondering why you aren't as successful as you desire, start by taking stock of your habits.

The people whose lifestyle, money, success, and fame you most likely admire are the ones who awake at 5 am, run a few miles, meditate, have a fresh juice for breakfast, set tasks for the day – basically get shit done. You'll seldom find them surfing aimlessly on the web, binge-watching Netflix or refreshing their social media feed endlessly. They are constantly are work, either actually working or learning about ways to be more effective at work.

Every minute of their waking time is devoted towards being productive. They are feverishly working towards their destiny, building one block at a time.

Tell me something. Are you satisfied with where you are currently in your life? Have you truly achieved the success and glory you deserve? Are you living your dreams or simply existing on auto-pilot? If not, it's time for some major reprogramming and changes in everyday habits. You'll be stunned by how much can be accomplished by making tiny, gradual changes in your everyday habits, thought patterns and mindset.

I am not talking some self-help humbug that looks good only on paper. I am talking real, actionable, practical, doable steps that can help you scale unimaginable heights. These are habits people have used to transform their life 360 degrees. By adopting these power-packed 20 habits, you will unlock the key to your true success and glory. You will unleash your fullest potential to lead a successful, wealthy and glorious life.

These habits are designed to streamline efforts, instill more discipline in your life, and help you accomplish their success you deserve. They are proven to boost your energy, productivity, passion and enthusiasm towards your goals.

Are you still stuck with making a fast buck using one of the tons of crappy get rich quick schemes out there? Let me break the bubble. It doesn't work! Build get-rich sure careers and businesses that will help you build long-term wealth, which will take time, patience, consistent efforts and endless reserves of perseverance. True success and wealth creation need channelization of your energy towards businesses that last.

The transformation from nothing to everything is a result of self-discipline, efforts and consciously channelized efforts. Once you begin to witness even tiny results, you'll be motivated to keep going. Success and results (however small) are the biggest drivers for even more success, wealth and results.

Building self-discipline is like building a muscle. The more you keep training it, the stronger and more formidable you become. The less you train and nurture it, the weaker and less effective you become. We all have muscular strength. Similarly, all of us possess self-discipline. Much like each person's muscular strength varies; people possess different degrees of self-discipline. Though everyone has it, not everyone has developed it. It takes muscle to create and grow more muscle.

Similarly, it takes self-discipline to grow greater self-discipline. Have you used progressive weight training technique to build muscle? It is about lifting weights gradually until you can no longer lift anything more. You push your body's muscles until they give in and finally, rest. There's always scope for more.

This is similar to how self-discipline works. You build discipline by dealing with challenges that can be successfully achieved, but they are still near the limit. This doesn't translate into trying and failing each day at something new. It also doesn't imply staying in your cushy comfort zone. You don't gain strength by attempting to lift weight that cannot be budged nor do you gain strength by lifting weights that are increasingly light. You begin with weights/challenges that are within your current ability, but they are also near your optimal limit.

In Progressive training, you keep increasing the challenge. If you stay within your comfort zone and keep working with the same weight capacity, you aren't getting any stronger buddy. Likewise, if you don't put yourself to test in life periodically, you don't gain self-discipline. Like a majority of people don't develop their muscles to their fullest potential with proper training, most people do not boast of high discipline levels.

Avoid pushing yourself too much when it comes to building self-discipline. That's not the best way to go about it. You can't transform your life 360 degrees in a day. It isn't realistic to go from slack king/queen to productivity ninja overnight. You can't set three dozen goals, and expect yourself to meet each of them consistently from the next day. It's a recipe for disaster. It is similar to a person hitting the gym for the first time and aiming to pack 300 pounds. It doesn't work and makes you look foolish!

If you can start with 15 pounds, so be it. There's nothing to hide or be ashamed of. You begin now and from where you currently are. No matter where you are with your discipline (even highly undisciplined), start. Begin with little self-discipline to build even more discipline. As you get stronger with discipline, the weights or challenges will seem much lighter.

Avoid comparing yourself with others. It will never work. Your expectations will be even harder to meet. If you believe you aren't strong, everyone will appear much stronger. Just look at where you currently are and aim to improve as you move ahead.

Let's us look at an example to understand this better. Assume you want to be able to put in 9 solid hours of productivity at work every day because you are aware that this will make a positive impact on your career. Plenty of our office time is spent socializing and indulging in unproductive vices. So obviously there is plenty of scope for improvement where your goal is concerned.

To begin with, you start working for 9 hours with distractions and can manage to accomplish this only once. You are a disaster the next day. You can do one round of 9 hours for a day but not more. So, let's cut back now. What duration will be able to sustain successfully for going an entire week? How about working with complete focus for an hour a day, five days in a row? Doable? If not, how about half an hour a day, five days in a row? Start with whatever you are comfortable with. If you think it's too easy a task, increase the challenge. The idea is to make it a mix of challenging and doable. Something that is an easy enough to be practical and challenging enough to inspire you.

Once you've work uninterrupted for an hour for a week, take it to next level during the subsequent week. Continue to persevere with the progression until you reach your goal of 9 productive hours each day. You are raising the bar gradually each week instead of doing it all at once, which doesn't sustain in the long run. Stay within your capability while also growing stronger. Once you build self-discipline, you slowly enjoy the benefits of everything you've done in the long haul. The training indeed produced value that makes your life more fulfilled, rewarding and gratifying. There are plenty of ways to build your self-discipline muscle, which you can get started with right away.

Chapter One:

Powerful Goal Setting Secrets

Keep your vision on the bigger picture

If you are working in an organization, are you simply concerned about coming to office, getting your work and returning home? This isn't exactly the best recipe for success.

Do you know your organization's corporate strategy? Do you know its revenue model? How about its long-term vision? Don't be wedded to short-term goals or act myopically. Always keep your eye on the bigger picture when it comes to setting goals.

Even while setting your business goals, keep a close eye on the bigger picture. What do you eventually want to accomplish with the business? Why are you doing this in the first place? Marrying strategy, long-term vision, and goal planning are vital to accomplishing success. What do you need to do to keep your employees happy, productive and fulfilled? What will make your customers happy?

What is your ultimate aim in life? Most people seek to be financially free to live fulfilling, rewarding and gratifying life. Being financially free in its truest sense is having all the time in the world and all the money in the world to enjoy it. Some people have all the time in the world but no money to enjoy it. Others have all the money in the world but no time to enjoy their money. True financial freedom is about having both - the time to enjoy your money and the money to spend in your free time. Is your ultimate goal of financial freedom? Or do you want to accomplish something else?

I know some youngsters who want to retire at 40 and travel the world. This drives them to work hard and give it their all each day.

Keep the bigger picture in mind. This will award you greater clarity and focus when it comes to putting your goals into action. It will drive you to be more disciplined and dedicated to your work.

The bigger picture includes both - what has been and what's the future like. Use your creativity and go deep into developing the bigger picture. I've had several people come to me and ask me how to work out their bigger picture or even goals that lead to the bigger picture.

Here are some ways to create your goal big picture.

Free writing thinking and drawing. If someone gave me a penny each time my thought wandered, I'd be a multi-millionaire with my own private plane, yacht - the works. However, some of my most creative insights occur while thinking freely. Tap into your creativity to figure out your goals and the bigger picture. Ideas can't be right or wrong, correct or incorrect! Don't judge ideas or expect them to be too realistic/practical. Carry your notebook or phone.

Jot down ideas as they occur to you. It can be while driving, walking, watching television, seeing a hoarding on the street, showering and so on. Ideas can strike anywhere, be prepared to record them or lose them forever. Create an atmosphere for maximizing your creativity. I like the idea of setting up a personal creativity zone in the house or outside patio. Play some soft music and get the free-thinking process beginning. Don't worry about how silly or good your ideas are - just get them flowing. What do you want to do?

What are the different possibilities of doing it? For instance, you may want to make money by traveling the world. What are the different ways through which you can fulfill this? What is the big picture of your goal? Do you want to lead a more adventure-packed and exciting life? Do you want to stay away from a 9-5 job? Do you want to create something of interest to people that urge them to give you their regular, average life and travel? Some people like to draw their ideas instead of writing them. Sketch or doodle your ideas. Draw a bigger goal or your big picture and surround it with smaller sub-goals. The idea is to clarify what you want to by keeping fixated on the bigger picture before you actually get down to doing it.

Chunk your big goal into smaller sub-goals

Though your eyes should be on the bigger picture or the true purpose of doing something (remember your 'whys?'), don't take your eyes off the next step. The most important step in the process of any goal fulfillment is the subsequent step. Imagine being given the task of climbing the world's tallest mountain. If you look at the summit, you'll be fairly intimidated. You'll never believe you can scale a mountain that high! It seems like a daunting task if you view summit from the base. The summit seems unattainable and virtually impossible to scale.

You'll be more confident of reaching the camp a few feet above the base than the summit because the camp appears way closer than the summit. Can you reach the base camp? Undoubtedly yes! You'll reach it fairly quickly and easily. Once you cover the base camp, look at the subsequent camp located 400 feet above the current camp.

Do you think you can reach there? Of course, you can! It is only 400 feet above this one, no big deal. You keep looking at the next step each time until you access the final summit. This should be your approach towards success, money, and life mastery goals too. Keep your eyes firmly fixated on the subsequent goal or camp rather than fearing the final goal or summit.

When we think about a massive goal, we may feel intimidated or overwhelmed by the task of accomplishing it. This isn't to say you shouldn't set big, ambitious goals. By all means, know where you want to reach, but keep your vision on the next step to make it seem more realistic and attainable. Once we move past a camp, our confidence in our ability to reach the summit increases. With each step you climb or every small goal you accomplish, your faith in accomplishing the bigger goal increases.

Have you read Brain Tracy's *Focal Point?* It refers to a technique that if applied can bring about a huge transformation in the way you approach goals. The author mentions that if you feel overwhelmed by your goals, focus on finishing the initial 10 percent of the tasks required to fulfill the goal. When you perform 10 percent of the tasks required to accomplish a goal, you gather the momentum to continue. Once you gain momentum by simply beginning doing one-tenth of the task, you are likelier to complete it. Try it, it works wonders.

Let us say you want to create an information-rich social media pages with a thousand quality posts. Now obviously, you can't create all thousand posts in a day or even week. However, if you make a list of all the topics that you'd like the posts to be related to or a rough idea for each post, you've completed 10 percent of the task. This step will decrease the gap between you and your goals and get you into action-mode. Aim to finish 10 percent of each task, to begin with, before scheduling a timeline for finishing the remaining tasks.

Make visual maps for goals. Let's say you want to chunk bigger goals into smaller pieces of attainable, realistic tasks. How do you go about breaking the larger goals into sub-goals? I know writing goals seemed so last year, yet it is important from the goal internalizing perspective (in the next chapter). However, I have a more exciting, interesting and upgraded version! It is called visual maps.

Visual maps are very effective when it comes to creating goals and committing them to paper. Start by drawing a huge circle in the middle of a paper. In the middle of this circle, mention your ultimate goal. It can be anything from being a multi-millionaire to be being the best fashion boutique owner in the city to converting a hobby you are passionate about into a highly profitable profession.

Let's say you want to convert your cake baking skills into a highly profitable business venture. In the middle of the large circle, you'll mention this goal. Next, draw lines originating from the large circle about all that needs to be done to accomplish your goal. In the above example, you may search for cake baking gigs online or in the local newspaper. You may ask your family, friends and social contacts for references of people who may be interested in your cake baking services. You may launch social media pages and accounts to showcase your skills and connect with prospective clients. You may also proactively get in touch with companies and organization that you think may need cakes.

You get in touch with wedding planners or leave your cards at jewelry stores selling engagement rings and wedding bands. You may also connect with to-be brides and grooms to understand if they have any requirement for cakes. How about sprucing up your LinkedIn profile? Now, you can view everything you need to do to fulfill your goal on a single page. Mention everything that needs to be done to reach that one big goal you have there in the middle.

Create timelines for sub-goals. Let us say you are entering a burger eating challenge in the newest restaurant in town. The burgers are predictably monstrous and massive. It's almost impossible to push the giant-sized burgers down your throat all at once. What will be your strategy if you have to eat the maximum burgers possible? Will you able to accomplish the desired results if you just put them in your mouth as a whole? Probably not! How about breaking it into smaller pieces that are easier to gobble? Converting it into bite-sized pieces will make the burger easier to swallow, and you may end up eating much more.

It is pretty much the same story with our goals. Think of your seemingly impossible goals as the giant-sized burger that cannot be gobbled in one shot. However, it is an altogether different story if you break into easier to swallow and digest bits. You cannot fulfill a big goal in one shot. Hats off if you can though! However, most people need to break their big goals into smaller pieces or sub-goals to fulfill them.

Chunk bigger and near impossible goals into smaller, more accomplishable parts for boosting your chances of accomplishing them. This way, instead of a single big goal you are dealing with several tinier goals, which may not seem like a very daunting task.

For instance, let us say your ultimate goal is to learn to play the guitar. Are you going to be a guitar maestro in a day? You'll start by buying a guitar first, followed by probably signing up for guitar classes/lessons. The learning sessions may start by picking up elementary music scales. Later, you'll graduate to intermediate scales. Finally, you may master the most advanced scales.

All along, create a schedule of the deadline for each sub-goal, so you stay on track with the final goal. Avoid having a single deadline for the entire goal. This way you are more likely to slip into procrastination mode. I create smaller milestones for each goal to help me stay inspired and motivated. Instead of looking at the monstrous burger and wondering how you can eat it all in one shot, looking at smaller pieces makes the ultimate goal come across as more realistic and achievable.

Each time you accomplish a smaller milestone you feel inspired to keep going in the direction of the bigger goal. Not just larger goals, this principle can be followed in daily tasks too. Let us say you have to complete a presentation comprising 50 slides in the next five days. Instead of relaxing for the first 2-3 days and then working at feverish pace to complete it within the next 2 days, break the bigger goal into smaller sub-goals of 10 slides a day. This way you will be on track with your bigger goal of 50 slides at the end of 5 days. The tendency is to hold off until the last minute is a huge productivity killer. Keep yourself accountable for finishing smaller sub-goals by breaking down the final deadline into smaller timelines.

You can't arise one day and suddenly say I will stop smoking today after years of chain smoking. Again, it's wonderful if you can, but that isn't how it works for most people. You can start by going without nicotine for a few hours, then probably a day, followed by a couple of days. This can then help you gain the confidence of creating even bigger goals like going smoke-free without a few weeks, months and then finally years.

If you start by saying you will stop smoking forever at the onset, you'll feel largely overwhelmed and doubtful about the idea. It seems big, unrealistic and impossible (remember the animal burger). However, if you just think about going smoke-free for a day or couple of days, the idea of giving up doesn't seem so bad and unattainable after all.

It is also important to prioritize sub-goals. Let us assume you are studying for a bachelor's degree, which is the bigger goal here. Now we break this big goal into several bite-sized goals (the various papers/subjects you need to tackle to earn your degree). You most likely won't have to work equally on all papers. You may be more expert in one paper/topic than another.

Identify your areas of weakness. Which of the sub-goals need more attention than others? Which of the sub-goals can act as an obstacle when it comes to accomplishing the overall goal? This paper will gain precedence over others regarding priority. You don't want it to lower your overall score, which means you'll spend more time on the particularly challenging paper/topic. This challenging paper/ topic may need to be tackled first. It may need more time, attention and focus than other papers. It is your priority sub-goal. You may be scoring well in other papers, which means you may not need to work as hard on them as papers where your scores can be improved.

Prioritize sub-goals by time, attention, focus, importance, urgency and so on in the overall goal fulfillment process.

List what's required to accomplish each sub-goal

Once you have broken a large goal into smaller, bite-sized sub-goals, created a timeline for sub-goals and identified priority sub-goals, go over what exactly is needed to fulfill each sub-goal.

Let us say for example you want to quit your day job and make money by pursuing your passion for photography. What are the things you'll need to convert your passion into a rewarding and steady source of income?

You'll have to start by polishing your resume and LinkedIn profile to include photography projects you've worked on in the past. You may have to ask people within your social circle for leads and references. Then, probably create your social media blogs/pages to showcase your portfolio.

You may connect with organizations/companies that offer freelance assignments to photographers to build your portfolio. You may look for event gigs in your neighborhood or run through newspaper and online classifieds about photography gigs offered in the city.

What are the actual tasks needed to achieve every sub-goal? Let's say your first sub-goal is working on your social media profile and resume. You may start by looking at the social media pages of other photographers. What are their style and USP? How do they market their services? How do they engage their followers? How do they close deals? You'll identify the terms and images professional photographers use of their social media to gain the required audience traction. What information and terms can you use in your resume to make it impressive? You'll probably mention a photography certification or course you recently completed or a photography related college project that garnered you plenty of appreciation as an upcoming photographer.

Think about every step or action required to fulfill each sub-goal. Go over practical to-do tasks, learning/reading and other aspects that will be needed to put it into action.

Let us consider another example. Your primary goal is boosting your GPA score. What will be the different steps required for achieving this goal? You may have to put aside all distractions and schedule extra study hours every day. Then, maybe you'll take coaching lessons a couple of times during the week. You may also have to devote time for additional reading.

Once the sub-goals have been identified, plan a strategy for tackling each sub-goal. The first sub-goal is to dedicate extra hours for studies. What do you need to do to accomplish this sub-goal? Reduce television time, cut down on gaming, turn off social media notifications.

The next sub-goal is to sign up for special coaching lessons. You may need to give your weekend dance lessons or sports practice to make way for additional coaching. Then, find a competent and experienced tutor who can guide to improve GPA score. You may have to go over a list of tutors in your locality to get in touch with each of them. We are creating a plan of action for each sub-goal that helps us accomplish the ultimate, bigger goal.

Get the idea? All these sub-goals originate from the larger goal of wanting to convert your passion into a money-making profession. Now you don't just have sub-goals – marketing, cold-calling, building a profile, seeking gigs and so on but you've also listed the tasks that need to be done to fulfill every sub-goal.

Measure, Review and Evaluate Goals Periodically

Measure, review and evaluate your goals are frequent intervals to check where you are placed in the context of the overall goal. Where do you presently stand where the bigger goal is concerned? At times, measuring goals will be a challenge, in which case you'll simply need to keep recording results and measure them against the bigger goal.

Let us assume your goal is anger management. You want to prevent and control anger bursts and fits that are causing a lot of distress in your life. To begin with, your goal is to prevent bursting into fits for anger for the next one year. How can this be measured? Maintain a record of all instances where you experienced an overpowering urge to fly into a fit of rage but resisted the urge. This can be done daily or weekly. Record the time number of times you gave in to the anger impulse. How many times did you resist from giving in to your angry spells? How many times did you succumb to venting your anger? What did you say or do in anger? Was the emotion justified or did you simply act in impulse? Did you misplace someone else's anger elsewhere?

Go through these questions at the end of the day. You keep measuring, reviewing and evaluating your goals periodically to stay on track. Some goals are more exactly measurable. It is easier to record your progress. If you've signed up for a degree and complete each paper to earn the degree, you know where you stand when the papers are evaluated. You know exactly how much you've scored in each module. Evaluation of progress is easier.

Likewise, if your goal is to become lighter by 50 pounds, it is easier to track and record your progress each week by determining how many pounds you've managed to knock off. Not all goals are as easy to measure. You may not be able to measure them precisely. I mean, how can you tell the exact levels by which your rage has reduced? You'll, therefore, have to depend on recording things to evaluate progress made so far into the goal.

In the anger management example, how many times did you resist screaming at someone or something? Which was the last instance when you threw a fit of rage without any apparent reason? How do you vent your anger currently? Is there any noticeable change in the nature and frequency of the way you express your anger? Recording progress is critical to the process of goal fulfillment as it helps you stay on track, and work your way through the goal in a focused and mindful manner.

If you feel things aren't going as planned, reviewing your progress may help modify your strategy. For example, let us say your goal is to lose a specific amount of weight. If you keep reviewing and measuring your goal periodically, you may realize that you are not losing the intending amount of weight at the given intervals. This may require a change in the diet plan or replacing ineffective supplements. You may end up switching to another diet plan or increase the duration and intensity of your physical workout to accomplish the desired results.

One of the biggest advantages of measuring and reviewing your goals frequently is that you can take a slight detour or modify your strategy to accomplish your goals more effectively each time you go off track or do not get the desired results. If you go off the track, you can get back with a newer approach.

I know people who create goal journals to track and record their progress. For instance, a tally of how many times they resisted smoking or drinking alcohol throughout the week/month if their goal is to give up smoking and drinking.

Create an accountability blog

If you are famous for making grand plans and never implementing them, a proven 'castles in the air' champ, a day-dreaming ninja, this is exactly what you should do to push yourself into action. To move from procrastination to productivity, start an accountability blog and gain as many followers as you can. Once you have a bunch of people following you and closely watching your actions, you are less likely to give up.

Plus, knowing that your actions are inspiring and influencing them to follow suit will prevent you from throwing in the towel. Chronicle your journey on a blog. Where did you start? How far have you reached in the journey of goal accomplishment? What have you done to overcome challenges along the way? Admit it; none of us wants to be seen as someone who isn't true to their word. The fact that you hold yourself accountable for your goal fulfillment journey tells yourself and others and that you are here to stay!

An accountability blog will help you

-Document and track your progress. It's a wonderful way to view and assess how far into the journey you've actually arrived.

-Keep yourself inspired, motivated, positive and accountable for your actions. Knowing that you will be sharing your entire journey with your followers helps you stay on track. You'll think twice before giving up your goals because obviously, you don't want to be seen as someone who fails or backing downs or doesn't practice what they preach. I would want people to cheer me and applaud my progress/success along the way. In reality, you are audaciously letting the world known about your nearly impossible goals, which is a huge motivator (works like a charm for me). I wouldn't want to back down or fail, which will keep pushing you to do your best all the time. You can get an accountability partner on board, so you both watch out for each other while fulfilling your goals.

-You can share plenty of your own tips, strategies, ideas, and techniques for accomplishing goals. You may have learned of a faster, smarter, more sustainable or better way to do something from experience, which is wonderful sharing. Think of it as offering value to your readers or giving it back to society. You'll be amazed at how much you can share.

-Motivate others who are sailing in the same boat as you. The accountability blog can help people who are pursuing the same goals or are in a similar stage/situation. It's good to know aren't the only one. Popular accountability bloggers receive several emails and blog comments from readers sailing in the same boat urging them for help and suggestions. With your positivity and upbeat spirit, you can encourage others to enthusiastically chase their goals.

-Who knows? You may end up making nice profits from the blog!

Keep them detailed and specific

The more specific, unambiguous and detailed your goals, the brighter are your chances of achieving them. Be open, practical and realistic while setting goals. When you don't have clear goals, you are less likely to embark on the right path. If you want a pay hike, state exactly how much you want your pay to rise by. Simply saying an increase won't have the desired effect. If you want to boost your business profits in the next six months, state exactly how much you grew by! You'll give yourself direction by doing so.

If your goal is to earn passive income amounting to $15,000 a month within the next six months, you know precisely what investments you need to make that much. You'll need to access incoming income from your businesses and other ventures. What are the chances you'll act in the right direction if you don't know exactly what you want?

Let us say you are a travel blogger. If your goal is to earn a steady income from the blog, you need to have a precise figure in mind to work on it. How will you know how many affiliate marketing programs to sign up for? How many advertisers to target? How many information products to create? You won't know what all you need to do unless there is a clear figure in mind. Compare this with knowing that you need to make $3000 from the blog to in the next six months. Then, you divide it into $1500 from affiliate commissions, $500 from eBook sales and $1000 from direct advertising.

This will give you a rough idea about how many organizations to approach, the number of emails you'll need to send each day, the volume of content that has to be created and the number of readers/followers you'll need to reach your magic figure. Get the drift? Specific goals lead to specific actions in the required direction. If you are dealing with vague and open goals, you aren't setting yourself up for success.

Set Priorities

Each time you face a different football team, you are setting yourself up for different obstacles. Not all teams will have the same strategy. Some will have a powerful defense that will stop you in the tracks, while others will boast of a great offense slicing through your defenses to score. The game is won by observing and identifying the opponent's strategy. Based on this strategy, you will utilize your limited resources or player optimally to win the game.

The game of life is not much different. You have limited resources at your disposal when it comes to accomplishing your goals. The key to winning the game of life is to prioritize your tasks and actions. If your opponent has a power-packed defense, you will have to strategize and establish priorities to move past their scrimmage line. Similarly, if the opponent has a powerful offense, your defense must be equally strong. The secret is to bring the right team on the field to tackle the opponent's strategy. This is where the people you surround yourself with make all the difference.

Set priorities and get in the right bunch of players. Being weak in any one area will give the opponent a chance to attack your weakness, leading to defeat. Prioritize while setting goals. Learn to say no to games and players that do not help you win the game or move ahead. Weight every player against a list of priorities and do a quick check of where they fit with your priorities. This is a simple and efficient way to move ahead with your goals. Simply throwing players randomly into the game is a recipe for disaster.

Then, you must also have a coach who helps you succeed with your goals. A person who knows the game inside out, and has played with a winning strategy! Even the best quarterbacks struggle without a competent coach. Have a person to a group of people help you strategize while setting goals. Pick the best players, coach, and strategy by setting priorities. You are setting yourself up for victory by laying down your priorities.

Chapter Two:
Internalize Your Goals

Do you know you have a magic weapon that can help you accomplish everything you want? Yes, practically everything! It can help you fulfill all your objectives, desires, goals and visions. The magic tool is capable of converting your thoughts into tangible things. Your ideas into reality! Your visions into your destiny! This all-powerful and potent tool is none other than your subconscious mind.

Our subconscious mind has the potential to fulfill all our desires. It has the power to absorb ideas we feed into it and guide our actions in alignment with these ideas. The superpower of our subconscious mind is it cannot differentiate between the real and the imagined. For instance, if you keep visualizing yourself as a rich and successful person, the mind doesn't recognize this as wishful thinking. It firmly believes this to be your reality.

Once the subconscious mind believes something to be real, it leads your actions in line with you it believes. If your mind believes you are a rich and successful go-getter, it will seize opportunities, come up with ideas and lead you to act in the direction of success. You have the power to create everything you desire with the help of your subconscious mind.

The human mind consists of three layers, the conscious, subconscious and unconscious mind. While the conscious mind is a realm we are fully aware of, we have almost no awareness of the thoughts, feelings, emotions, beliefs, and ideas held within subconscious and unconscious (which is what makes it so powerful).

Thus, we often hold certain strong positive, negative, self-limiting and empowering ideas within our subconscious unknowingly. Since this realm of your mind remains inaccessible, you don't know what thoughts and beliefs are held in it, which are impacting your actions.

However, the good news is – you can start feeding empowering and positive ideas to your subconscious mind by internalizing your goals. When you internalize your goals, the subconscious mind believes it to be your reality. When it believes something to be your ultimate reality, it guides your actions in alignment with these positive and empowering thoughts.

You possess all the resources and tools to make a roaring success of your life. You have the potential to manifest any goal or dream because you choose what you feed into your subconscious mind.

Chances are you've already heard about Rhonda Byrne's book and movie *The Secret?* If no, here's a quick summary. It is based on the law of attraction, which borrows from multiple fields of study such as quantum physics, metaphysics, psychology, spirituality and more. In short, the law of attraction states that we can create our reality through our thoughts, which are believed to hold powerful energy frequencies. When we transit these thoughts into the realm of the universe, the universe energy (or atomic mass of energy held within the universal space and time) responds to our thoughts with a matching frequency to give us exactly what we want.

Think of yourself as nothing but a bundle of energy, pretty similar to everything in the universe. You act as an energy magnet, which thought-feelings, thoughts, emotions, and actions are attracting things in your life. When the universal atoms or energy receives these energy signals, it responds with a frequency match, and you receive exactly what you fixate your feelings and thoughts on.

This, unfortunately, works both ways. The universal energy cannot distinguish between the positive and the negative. It doesn't know what's good or not good for you. It simply responds at an energy level. I've had people come up to me and ask why despite the best efforts they aren't able to manifest their desires. The problem is easy to pin down.

A majority of times, we end up focusing on what we want to get rid of or what we want to avoid instead of what we want. When you focus on what you want to discard instead of what you wish to attract, you end up attracting even more of the unwanted because that's where your thought energy is concentrated.

Let's say I want to wealthy. My dream is to earn plenty of money and live a life free of insecurity, debt, and financial burdens. Instead of channelizing my thoughts in the direction of "being wealthy" if I focus on "don't want to be poor," I'll only end up attracting more poverty. The universe doesn't understand the difference between negatives and positives. It will give you what you ask for – so better focus on and ask for the right things. One of the most common reasons why we can't accomplish true success is because we focus on what we want to eliminate instead of what we want to magnetize in our life.

Remember, you have the key to fulfill your goals by reprogramming your mind, and transmitting the perfect energy signals to the universe.

How to use the law of attraction for your goal fulfillment

Visualization

Practice visualization techniques on awakening or before hitting the bed each day. Our subconscious mind is at its active best when the conscious mind rests while we are asleep. This is why most of our "aha moments" or "moments of solutions and realizations" happen while we are asleep.

Visualizing just before you go to bed helps you mind absorb these images clearly and work on them. Begin by sitting in a distraction-free space, which has a positive, relaxed and calming aura. Sit in a comfortable position and close your eyes. You will now imagine or visualize powerful images through your mind's eye.

Begin by visualizing what you want in absolute and vivid details. Remember, the more precise, detailed and unambiguous your visualization, the higher are your chances of manifesting it. You are telling your subconscious mind exactly what you desire to receive from a catalog of goodies. Make your visualization a multi-sensory process.

Let us say you are visualizing your dream office. Imagine it in explicit, graphics and multi-sensory details. How does the entrance of your office look? What is the logo and text on the board at the entrance? How does your workplace smell? What color are the walls? How are the tables, chairs and other furniture? What's the flooring like? How are the windows and doors like? Visualize everything in detail.

Similarly, if your goal is to make become a millionaire at the end of the year, visualize being a millionaire. How do you look as a millionaire? What are the clothes, footwear, and accessories you are sporting? How do people respond to you? How do people greet you when they meet you for the first time? How to do walk, talk, stand and express yourself?

By imagining all this in detail, you are allowing your subconscious mind to internalize these powerful goals and guide your actions in line with these goals. The most important aspect of visualization is to imagine them as if these are your reality (or as if they've already been fulfilled), happening in your life currently, not as something you want in future.

You must align your thought energy with the idea that this is indeed your reality. By going over these positive thoughts repeatedly, you are building powerful ideas and energy vibrations that invariably help you magnetize these things. Wishful thinking doesn't work because when you operate from the perspective of wanting something, you are confirming the lack of it in your life presently. However, when you operate from the perspective that something is already yours, you are simply drawing more of it.

For instance, let us say you want to be rich, and lead a financially secure and comfortable life. When you focus on wanting more, you are in effect stating that you don't have enough of it. Visualizing from this from a scarcity of wealth and prosperity perspective makes it even more scarce and unattainable.

However, if you operate from the perspective of already possessing plenty of wealth and prosperity, you are on your way to attracting more riches and a financially glowing fortune. Imagine, visualize and internalize the emotions and feelings of achieving your goals. Practice visualize for a minimum of 10 minutes two times a day.

When you strongly imprint strong ideas of being of being rich, successful and productive in your subconscious mind, your program is for recognizing and seizing opportunities that create even greater wealth and success (or other goals you may have).

Focus your thoughts on positivity, action, gratitude, and prosperity, while eliminating negative, self-limiting and anxious thoughts that act as obstacles to your success.

By concentrating on what you desire as if you already own it, you are tuning your mind to new possibilities, perspectives, and opportunities. Leverage the characteristic of your subconscious mind where the line between reality and imagined reality is blurred. Your feelings and emotions about the goals you desire to accomplish are the most powerful magnet when it comes to magnetizing these goals. Our feelings possess an energy that is communicating with the universe at an atomic level. Overpoweringly positive feelings about accomplishing your goal help you act in line with this belief.

Through the process of visualization, you are feeding tangible ideas to the subconscious mind or clear, conspicuous goals to work on. Visualization helps you identify and clarify your goals while keeping these images active in your subconscious to lead you into taking positive action in the direction of these goals.

By practicing consistent visualization, your thoughts, emotions, and feelings stay in alignment with your goals. This helps you stay motivated, positive and inspired. Visualization is a multi-disciplinary technique that can channelize your mental power to convert your goals or visions into tangible reality.

I also recommend combining the practice of visualization with mediation, deep breathing, and guided visualization (there are plenty of guided visualization videos on the internet).

One of the most important things to keep in mind when it comes to internalizing your goals through visualization is to view yourself as an active participant in it. Let's say you are viewing the movie of your life. However, you aren't just a passive audience who is watching events unfold before you. You are the main character, an active participant and an integral part of the movie. You visualize yourself living your goals in different settings. You feel, imagine and absorb all experiences, including the sensory ones.

Once your subconscious mind absorbs all goals, it'll be easier to work in line with these goals.

Affirmations

Affirmations are powerful positive statements that are uttered repetitively to help implant an idea or goal into the subconscious mind. This process then enables the subconscious mind to believe these ideas/goals, and align your actions in line with them. The key is to keep saying these statements aloud or writing them continuously for the subconscious to accept it as your ultimate reality.

When we say something repeatedly, our words have a tremendous impact on the subconscious mind. There are certain energy vibrations associated with specific words, which create either positive and empowering mental images or negative and defeatist images. The energy frequency we feed our mind through words and phrases we continuously use ultimately impact our actions. Thus, by feeding it empowering mental images, we are channelizing our subconscious mind for success, wealth and life mastery.

Start this right away. Begin by creating a positive statement about an aspect of your life you wish you change. For instance, if you want to develop a more proactive, go-getter attitude when it comes to recognizing and seizing opportunities, try saying, "I am a proactive and action-oriented person who is always ready to identify and embrace new opportunities."

Similarly, if you want to make money, your affirmation can be something along the lines of, "I am a powerful money magnet. Money comes to me effortlessly." If you want to develop greater confidence or self-assertiveness, say something like, "I am a self-assured, assertive and confident person who has command over people and situations."

Say your affirmations for a minimum of three times a day, 20 times each (60 times in total). You'll gradually begin to notice a change in the way you view yourself, your situation or your chances of success. There will be a greater feeling of positivity and confidence in fulfilling your goals. Check your feelings, beliefs, and emotions before sleeping each night. Do you notice a difference after using affirmations? Do you feel more aligned with your goals? Do you feel the positive energy of these highly potent words and phrases? Is there a greater sense of hopefulness, optimism and positive energy? The answer is a resounding yes!

Affirmations are designed to keep our subconscious mind to stay concentrated on our goals. They help keep the mind on track with empowering thoughts, ideas, and energy to restrict doubts, self-limiting beliefs, fears, and other negative thought energy vibrations. When we realize our true potential, we have the power to activate the dormant goal-fulfilling powers of our subconscious. Notice the changes when you start saying your affirmations. You'll begin to feel more enthusiastic, energized and inspired about accomplishing them. There has to be a positive transformation from within to experience a transformation outside.

Before creating your affirmations, focus on what exactly you want to accomplish. Clarifying our goal makes it easy to internalize the goal to accomplish exactly what we want. Also, keep all affirmations in the present tense. You shouldn't say them as something that you hope to accomplish in the future. It should be said as your current reality. For instance, "I am rich, wealthy and prosperous."

Similarly, do not use negative words or phrases. Your subconscious mind, as well as the universe, doesn't understand "no" "not" "never" etc. Instead of saying, "I don't want to be in debt" say "I am wealthy and financially-free." Focus on statements that assert what you want not what you wish to get rid of. Also avoid using words or phrases such as "I wish for," "I seek" or "I desire/want." This again shifts the focus to the lack of it in your life currently. Always affirm in the present, doing, thinking and being what you truly desire.

Be very specific about what you want. Imagine the universe to be a catalog of desires or wishes. If you place a vague order, you may not receive your product, or you'll end up receiving another product that you didn't want.

This is exactly how the universe responds to your desires. Keep your affirmations precise, unambiguous and to the point. If you want to increase your monthly income, simply stating that "my monthly income has risen" may not have the desired effect. Even a raise of $0.50 is an increase, right? Instead, if we say, "My monthly income has risen by $1000", we are giving our mind a clear figure to work with. Thus, the feeling that is earning $1000 more each month is internalized, driving our subconscious mind to work on the goal effectively. Mention your affirmations in exacts to boost your chances of accomplishing it.

Eliminate every ounce of doubt, uncertainty, and insecurity held within you while chanting your affirmations. The intention should be positive and hopeful. Do not let your mind be overcome by fear of failure or other negative thoughts. You must believe these statements to be your truth for the law of attraction to work. A highly positive and potent energy frequency will be sent into the universe when you say these statements with a powerful intention. We must also believe that we are truly deserving of the wealth, success and mastery that we desire. Our goal magnetizing energy increases when we believe ourselves to be worthy of receiving everything we want.

There are tons of examples where people do not enjoy fulfilling and healthy interpersonal relationships in life or always end up falling in love with the wrong people and getting hurt repeatedly. If they do a mental check-in, they'll realize the root cause. They do not believe they deserve to be a loving and healthy relationship, to begin with. When we don't believe you deserve something, we are blocking its energy into our life by creating negative thought energy around it.

Do not block the energy for magnetizing your goals by doubting your worthiness to accomplish it. The best time to say your affirmations is when you are facing the mirror while shaving, applying make-up, getting dressed and so on. Observe the feelings, expressions and energy vibrations your experience while saying your affirmations.

I also like to stick my affirmations in places where I can prominently spot it throughout the day. There are these colorful, little post-it notes that have my affirmations on them, which I've stuck throughout my home and office. I read them mentally or aloud each time I come across them. You can stick your affirmations on the bathroom mirror, refrigerator, kitchen cabinets, cupboards, computer, and work desk – just about any place where you can see them several times in a day. We are doing nothing but embedding these ideas in our subconscious mind to draw it into action mode.

Feel the energy and emotions of your words while saying them rather than chanting them in a mechanical, auto-pilot manner. Internalize the emotions and feelings attached to the words. For example, if you state you are a money magnet which is forever attracting wealth and riches, soak in the emotions of being rich and prosperous. This is the key to activating the power of your subconscious mind and the law of attraction.

Journaling

Journaling is another powerful habit if you want to fulfill your life goals. The physical act of writing sends intensely strong signals to our subconscious to bring our actions in line with what we write.

Keep a goal, gratitude, dream or stream of consciousness journal. Gratitude is one of the most power-packed emotions when it comes to multiplying your blessings. In the book *Magic,* bestselling manifestation author Rhonda Byrne writes about the power of gratitude and thankfulness in attracting our goals or increasing more of the good things we possess.

Do this small exercise starting today. Mention a list of ten things that happened during your day that you are grateful for before going to bed each night. You can also create a list of ten things that you are blessed to have in your life each night. Ensure that it's a different list each day without any repetitions. Each day, challenge yourself to come up with ten new things that you are thankful for. Think there aren't that many? You'll be surprised.

Mention everything from your eyes to your Wi-Fi connection to the roof above your head to your hands to the food – there's a lot to be thankful for. Irrespective of your present situation, be thankful for all you have. When we express thankfulness for what we already have, we transmit powerful, positive energy into the realm of the universe, which true to its nature sends us even more of what we are thankful for.

If you want to attract more wealth, express gratefulness for your current wealth! If you want a pay hike, begin by being thankful for what you currently make.

Imagine your blessings while mentioning them in the gratitude journal. Thank the universe or any other force of your choice for these blessings while writing them. Similar to affirmations and visualizations, journal your goals as if they are already fulfilled.

We invest most of our time soaking in our problems and challenges. Understand that problems are a huge sign of life, that you are living and doing things. Perhaps the only time someone is problem-free is when they are six feet beneath. Shift focus from your problems to blessings. If you want to attract things you are grateful for, begin by expressing gratitude for existing blessings. Be grateful for everything, including your problems and challenges.

Gratitude is the biggest pathway to happiness, glowing health and success. It shifts our energy and attention from what we lack to what we have, which in turn helps us materialize greater blessings. It's the abundance of small pleasures, joys, and opportunities that we take for granted.

Write how it feels to accomplish your goals, the feelings, and emotions you experience after accomplishing your goals, and other details in the present tense. The subconscious mind will believe everything to be true, and help you act in line with your writings. Thus, your actions are guided by a more proactive and action-oriented thought process.

One of the most effective ways to unravel feelings, emotions, and thoughts held in our subconscious (often the self-limiting beliefs, fears and insecurities we hold within our subconscious prevents us from accomplishing our goals) is to write in a stream of consciousness. Write thoughts that freely flow through the stream of your consciousness without restraining, editing or assessing them. The act should be more intuitive and spontaneous, almost like an involuntary and uncontrollable impulse. You'll be surprised to learn about the thoughts, ideas, and beliefs held in your subconscious.

I also recommend keeping a dream journal handy next to your bed to tap into the subconscious. As soon as you awake after a dream or in the morning, start writing about your dream in detail along with the feelings you experienced while going through it. The idea is to put everything on paper before you forget it. Identify if there's a recurring pattern through your dreams. Accessing the ideas held in your subconscious through your dreams gives you the power to modify these ideas and beliefs if they aren't in line with your goal fulfillment.

Once our conscious realm takes precedence on awakening, the thoughts and ideas of the subconscious fade away, which is why it is important to note down your dreams quickly. Observe if there are any negative, defeatist or self-limiting thought patterns revealed through your dreams? Is there a recurring theme in a majority of your dreams? These are most likely our innermost thoughts, ideas and beliefs that stop us from accomplishing our goals. The transition from procrastination or inaction to hustling or productivity becomes smoother when you replace negative and self-limiting thoughts with positive, empowering and constructive ideas, thoughts, and beliefs. This is the key to internalizing your goals and donning the success mindset.

The habit of writing a daily journal is extremely therapeutic. It helps a person release negative thoughts such as regret, anger, low self-worth, stress, anxiety and so on. Releasing these thoughts is integral to the process of slipping into a more winning, goal-fulfilling mindset.

Journaling is a wonderful way to eliminate potential blocks that can come in the way of your goals.

Make your journal as personalized and relevant as you like. It should reflect your unique personality and goals. Add stickers, comic strips, movie quotes, lines from your favorite books, photographs, ticket stubs, feathers, sketches, doodles or anything that bets represents your goals to make the journal more personalized, meaningful and connect-worthy. You should feel an instant connection with your journal.

Don't simply write your goals and forget about it. The process of writing, of course, has plenty of advantages. However, go over your journal entries periodically to track your thoughts, feelings, beliefs, and emotions. You may notice a transformation in your thought patterns and beliefs. At the end of each week and month, go over all the entries for the particular week and month. Leave some space for reflecting on your progress.

Create a Vision Board

This one's my favorite. It now just helps you clarify your goals but also uses the power of your subconscious mind in manifesting these goals. Visuals have a strong impact on our subconscious mind. When it keeps seeing a visual or image repeatedly, the subconscious mind believes that to be your reality. It fantastically aligns your personal energy to the process of fulfilling your goals.

A vision board is a board that holds images or visuals of all your desires, goals, visions, dreams and objectives. Visuals are said to have a far more powerful impact on our subconscious than words. It is the difference between telling your mind what you want and showing it what you want. As simple! When our subconscious is exposed to a visual continuously, it internalizes the idea and believes it to be real. This helps our subconscious align our actions in line with these empowering visuals to facilitate goal fulfillment.

Be creative while making your vision board. It should be fun, personal and meaningful. Make a collage of images and photographs that resonate with your goals. It can be images from a catalog, brochure, magazine, internet, and comic strip – anything that symbolizes your goals pictorially. Select images that "talk to you" about your goals. Use your own photographs to reinforce goals. For instance, if you want to travel often, use a picture of one of your most memorable trips. The idea is to feed exactly what you want to accomplish in your subconscious mind. Who needs a genie with a magic lamp when you have your subconscious mind?

Place your vision board in a position where it's the first thing you see before you hit the bed and on waking up each morning. Place it on a wall opposite your bed. The vision board can also be placed above your work desk.

Notice how our conscious mind can seldom come up with solutions and ideas that the subconscious is capable of creating while we are asleep. Avoid picking pictures hurriedly or on a whim. Use only those visuals that resonate with you at a deeper level. Experience the emotions attached to these visuals, and feel them at a deeper level.

Avoid cluttering your vision board with too many images at once. Stick to four or five images at a time to help your mind focus clearly on them. You can also create a different vision board for each theme; say a wealth and career vision board, a relationship vision board and so on. Much like the journal, you can use a variety of elements to add more character to your vision board or personalize it. Souvenirs, tickets, pebbles, jewelry – anything that makes it unique, personal and stunning!

Turning negative self-talk into positive self-talk

Your mental chatter to a large extent determines your destiny. If this seems like an exaggerated statement – think again. Our subconscious is slowly but surely absorbing our mental conversations to create our thoughts, beliefs, ideas, and attitude. When you talk to yourself as a "loser, who can never get anything right" this is exactly what you are imprinting in the subconscious.

Again, it guides your action from this self-limiting and defeatist point of view. This is why it is said, "whether you think you can or you can't – you are right." This is because whatever you think is what your mind is going to create or lead you into doing. We blame everyone from the people we work with to our circumstances to our destiny for our failures without doing a mental check-in on the ideas we hold about self through our self-talk.

Worry not if they aren't exactly your own cheerleader. I've got your back covered there too. Here are some of the most powerful ways through which you can go from being a self-loathing critic to your biggest cheerleader.

1. Identify your thought patterns. What is the first thought that occurs to you when your boss

summons you and says he/she needs to speak to urgently. I am going to be fired? I must have done something really bad? The project that I submitted last evening is below his/her expectations? I mean you'd never really think, he/she's called you to ask if you are ready to accept more responsibility by taking up a big, upcoming project.

That's the thing about our thoughts. They are uncontrollable and involuntary. You don't have a mental leash to tame them. They automatically pop into your head without any effort.

From now on, I want you to closely monitor your inner dialogues. Take a few minutes to evaluate your conversation with yourself on a daily basis. Is there a clear pattern emerging through it? Do you always see yourself as a victim of circumstances? Do you always doubt your ability to do things? Do you think you are unworthy or incapable of accomplishing success and wealth? Are your opinions about yourself based on what other people think about you? There is almost always a clear underlying current in our negative self-dialogue. Recognizing this issue and eliminating it is the key to becoming your own cheerleader. Get into the habit of monitoring your habits consciously to identify unrealistic, irrational, self-limiting and unproductive thoughts.

2. Look for evidence of thoughts being true and untrue. Just because you think something doesn't necessarily mean it is true. Often our self-limiting beliefs, thoughts, and ideas are not facts but merely opinions. They aren't necessarily true. Each time you find yourself engaging in negative inner dialogue, look for evidence of its accuracy. Ask yourself, "What is the evidence that makes this thought true?" Going back to the above example, do you have evidence that your boss is going to fire you?

3. Make a list of all evidence that backs up your thoughts. You may have missed a crucial deadline or stayed absent from work for days due

to illness! List every reason why you think you are about to be fired.

Now create a list of reasons why your thoughts hold no value. You may be one of the team's most efficient and hardest workers. Clients request that you take on their projects because you are known to be a competent worker who delivers above average results! You've been called to meet the boss urgently on earlier occasions too without being fired.

If you have trouble coming up with evidence contrary to your negative chatter, ask yourself if you'd say the same thing to a close friend with the same issue. What would you say to him or her in a similar situation? If your friend calls and says, "Know what? I am about to be fired. What would your reaction be? You'll come up with a bunch of reasons why they won't be fired. Give yourself the same pep talk and consolation each time you find yourself engaging in negative self-talk.

4. Reframe your words and thoughts. When you've looked at a situation from both angles, create more realistic and less catastrophic statement about it. Instead of saying, "my boss wants to fire me because I goofed up on the last project" try telling yourself "yes, I goofed up on the last project, but there are several other reasons why my boss would want to talk to me." It'll help things stay in the right perspective.

I wouldn't recommend convincing yourself in too positive or glowing terms either when it comes to challenging negative self-talk. You'll know you are lying in you can't play football and think you are "the next Cristiano Ronaldo."

Stop thinking in extremes and look for more realistic thought patterns to move from inertia to productivity.

5. How bad is bad really? Okay so maybe your boss does want to fire you, or you may not succeed in your next business venture if you try. How bad is that? Spend a few minutes thinking about your response. Okay, maybe I am not good

at this. What does that mean? I can never be good at it?

The consequences are often not as drastic as we imagine them to be. Much like when someone doesn't respond to our calls or texts, in our signature catastrophic thinking patterns we believe the person is ignoring us or is with someone more interesting. Things aren't as bad a majority of the times. Negative thought patterns are wired in the human brain since evolution. Sensing danger and unfortunate events come to us easily. However, that doesn't mean everything bad is going to happen to you all the time.

Think about all the times you've not done something out of a compelling fear of failure. Didn't you regret it later when you witnessed others making a roaring success of it? Even if you fail, is it the end of the world? If you are fired, there are other companies and jobs to apply for.

If you fail at a start-up (you won't really know until you try, would you?), there are other businesses to venture into. You have options. Remind yourself that eventually, everything is alright. Put a pause on the anxiety, panic and worry button immediately.

You may never completely get rid of negative self-chatter, which is alright. The idea is to understand the brain's conclusions, remarks and predictions aren't always accurate, and our actions are often based on these inaccurate beliefs, conclusions or predictions. This way, you won't tend to be too affected by your negative self-chatter that often stirs up unproductive actions. The practice of replacing negative dialogues or self-talk with more positive ideas equips you to reach your fullest potential. You will less likely to be the best version of yourself if you keep talking down to yourself or beating yourself up mentally.

Avoid the urge to drag yourself down all the time, and instead make your mental chatter more productive, uplifting and realistic. This makes all the difference when it comes to internalizing your goals. Remember Brain Tracy's 10 percent rule? Just begin and accomplish 10 percent of your task to sustain the goal over a period of time. You are less likely to quit if you pick up the right momentum by completing 10 percent of the task.

Chapter Three:

Tackling the Procrastination Monster Head On

I may not know the perfect recipe for success but I sure as hell know the perfect recipe for failure – it's that funny little monster called procrastination. Think of all the wonderful things you could've accomplished by now but didn't owing to the tendency of putting things off for later. What's the rush? Why can't I do it later? Why can't I start my business after six months when I've learned more? Why can't I do this when the market becomes more promising? These are nothing but a bunch of excuses created by us to justify our inertia or inaction. Procrastination is the biggest enemy of productivity.

Think about this. It's Friday late afternoon and you the clock is ticking furiously. You are working on an assignment that has to be submitted before the day ends. You mentally whack yourself for not beginning sooner. Now you are focused simply on submitting the project on time, failing which you will be penalized. You hurriedly complete the project without focusing on quality. The end result - it's a complete mess. The project is sent back to you for rework.

Let us look at another scenario. You have an important presentation at work in the morning. Instead of getting your clothes and equipment ready the previous night, you fall asleep while playing console games or watching Netflix. You arise late the next morning because you forgot to set the alarm. Then, sleepy-eyed and irritable, you start looking for your clothes, only to realize that the clothes you planned to wear today aren't ironed. Now, there's no time to iron them because you also have to look for your pen-drive which you placed somewhere on the work table, which has a pile of papers that you planned to clear later in the week.

Now you wear the crumpled clothes after taking a quick shower and go looking for your pen drive. Finally, you find it only to realize there is no time for breakfast. You rush out without eating anything in crinkled clothes with the pen drive and laptop in your hand. Can you picture this potently negative and unfortunate scenario? You go to the office feeling tired, hungry and low on confidence. While making the presentation, you wonder if everyone is looking at your crumbled clothes and less than perfect appearance, which takes away the focus from everything you want to say? Needless to say, the presentation is a disaster.

Contrast this with getting things done on time. Wouldn't things have gone differently if you would've got things done on time? Wouldn't it be awesome if your clothes were neatly ironed and ready the previous day? Wouldn't it be great if you'd spend time reading through your presentation and having your equipment/devices in order instead of playing games? How about if you'd set the alarm and go to bed on time?

Wouldn't you awake feeling fresh, rejuvenated and ready to conquer the world? You would've made a stunning impression at the important presentation. Procrastination affects us in more ways than you realize. These seemingly small delays end up eating into your productivity and long-term success.

You have to spend time and energy on redoing the project. The time that you could've utilized for taking on other projects! If you are a habitual procrastinator, you aren't programmed for success. Period. Successful people several give in to short-term gratification by putting things off for later. On the contrary, they will delay short-term pleasures for long-term rewards.

Procrastination is the ultimate productivity killer. A trap that channelizes all your energies towards tasks that hold no value when it comes to working on your dreams and goals. Something that has the power to destroy your entire life if not taken by its horns!

Procrastination is generally mistaken for laziness, which it isn't. It is a more active process where we choose to perform one action instead of doing something we are aware we should be doing instead.

Laziness is inactivity or unwillingness to get into action mode, whereas procrastination involves ignoring seemingly unpleasant or inconvenient tasks that are important for more enjoyable pursuits. Instead of working on a project whose deadline is approaching, you choose to go out and enjoy a round of drinks with friends! Instead of studying for an important test, you find it more pleasurable to binge watch Netflix. I mean of course, Narcos and Stranger Things has more appeal than a bunch of letters and numbers adorning your books! Hello procrastinator!

Procrastinators or people who can't manage to delay gratification often witness little or no success in life. Make a note of some of the most successful people in their fields, and you'll notice that one trait that remains all-prevailing and common amongst them is their ability to delay short-term pleasures in return for long-term rewards. If you are focused on short-term pleasures, your idea of success is myopic.

It's an unfortunate cycle because every act of procrastination induces a sense of guilt, regret or shame in us, which leads to lower productivity and causes us to miss out on accomplishing important goals.

Over a period of time, procrastination can keep you demotivated, disillusioned and depressed about work. This can lead to businesses loses or losing your job in extreme cases. You don't want procrastination rearing its ugly head between you and goals.

You aren't a goal digger if you keep putting things for later. However, the good news much like all other monsters in your goal-fulfillment process, this one can also be slain.

Here are some ways to beat take the procrastination monster by its horns and beat it.

Avoid over-thinking and an obsession with perfection

I know some people who are such over thinking and over analyzing champs that they'd beat Sherlock Holmes or the FBI at their game. They think so much that their thoughts are seldom followed by concrete actions. Analyzing and thinking things through is good. The problem lies with excessive analyzing and thinking.

Let us say you want to create a money-making blog about parenting. Now, instead of focusing on different ideas and blog topics, you spend time thinking whether you'll have enough followers or they'll love your content, or there will be enough social media engagement, you are less likely to know what works and what doesn't. You are replacing potentially productive time that can be used for creating by over-thinking the idea until it suffocates and dies a slow death.

At times, we give projects more time than they deserve. We take much longer to finish things by becoming excessively hung up on tiny details. Most of us are guilty of this and let it pass under the garb of perfectionism. Let go of this urge to keep examining what you've done in the past, and instead get a major chunk of the work done, while finally revising things.

Confident, successful people are also overcome by doubts. However, they don't allow their doubts to grow into procrastination or delaying something out of fear or insecurity. Here are my pro hacks for side-stepping fear and doubt. Don't think in terms of all or nothing. A majority of people are somewhere in between, so you are not in as much danger as you imagine yourself to be. You may not make roaring profits, but you won't create an absolute turkey too. It's the law of averages.

Avoid setting impossibly high standards for yourself. It ends up disillusioning you if you don't accomplish those heights at the beginning itself. As we discussed in the earlier chapter, avoid catastrophizing or imagining the worst. Be mindful of your mental energy wastage. Instead of spending time thinking, overanalyzing and expending energy on trying to achieve over-perfect, just begin.

Once you start something, you can build your way through it and apply strategies based on trial and error. This is how you will accomplish perfectly. It won't come simply by reading everything you can about something, and then beginning it (unless you are planning to launch a rocket into space, in which case you should read everything). Jokes apart, perfection comes as you do things hands-on.

Let us go back to our earlier example about the parenting blog. Instead of over-thinking or over-analyzing, you simply start writing a few blog topic ideas and then fleshing them out into blog posts, you'll know what your readers dig. Getting to the task and knowing which way you are headed (and whether you need to change the course) is better than playing the guessing game. Let's say you create a few social media posts to promote your blog, but they don't get the desired response or engagement, you know you need to change your strategy.

Maybe, laser target your parents or people who may be interested in your content through paid advertising? Or maybe creating more opinion-based pieces that encourage people to share their instead of factual content that encourages passive reading? You get the point? Unless you do something, you won't know what works and what doesn't, and how to tweak things that don't work.

A solution, resourceful and out of the box thinking mindset comes only with doing not thinking. There's only so much you can accomplish by overthinking and analyzing things.

Perfection is often an everything or nothing mentality. We either want something to be perfect or fear to make a failure of it. People obsessed with perfect wait until everything is for them to begin. This simply means if it isn't perfect, it will not be done, which is unfortunate.

If we award yourself a penny for the number of times you've said you don't think this is the perfect time to do something, you'd probably be the world's richest or maybe second richest (if there's an even bigger procrastinator lurking around). You get the point?

This all or nothing mentality often holds us back. There is no perfect time for anything. The right time is when you begin. The idea is to start, and then make it right by working, modifying and reworking your strategies. Bold this if you want to, but unless you don't actually do something, you won't know if it works.

Focus on being more productive and effective than perfect. Instead of mentally striving for excellence, work on creating excellence or set yourself up with excellent conditions to get the task done. Remember, done is better than perfect. This isn't to say you shouldn't be worried about doing a task well, it just means you should stop using perfection as an excuse for inaction and get out of the all or nothing mindset to get shit done!

Make that someday who've been talking about today. Get started on your goal, and take pride in its accomplishment one step at a time.

Go back to your why

Remember we discussed the power of why at the beginning of the first book *Mindset of the Successful* in this bundle. Keep going to that why each time you find yourself sacrificing long-term rewards at the altar of short-term pleasures.

One of the most effective ways to deal with procrastination is to focus on long-term results. Procrastinators focus on short-term pleasures to duck the discomfort associated with performing a task. For them avoiding the effort of performing a task takes precedence over the consequences or stress of not performing it in the long run. What are the advantages of completing it? Go back to the benefits of accomplishing your long-term goals.

If you have been putting off studying for a degree than can help you get a better job or build a profitable business, consider the consequences of not getting the degree as opposed to the discomfort associated with studying for it. The so-called discomfort of studying is temporary, while the rewards of getting a degree are permanent.

Similarly, if you spend time in a more enjoyable pursuit instead of studying, you may enjoy short-term, temporary pleasures but you are nixing your long-term rewards in the bargain. Doesn't sound like a fair deal!

If you have been avoiding exercise because you think it is boring or there are other interesting and less physically strenuous things you can do in that time, think again! You are giving up glowing health, a fit body, loads of confidence and positive energy in the bargain. Again, it is a worthy deal?

Keep your eyes firmly on your "why" or real purpose for doing something each time you find yourself slipping into inaction. What is the most compelling reason you want to do something? For your family? For a cause, you truly believe in? For a life-long passion or mission? Your "whys" have the power to snap you out of inaction and get you into action mode.

If you want to live a financially free life by the time you are 40, what are you doing about it? Does your inaction and procrastination tally with your "why?"

Get a goal buddy

This works like magic when it comes to beating procrastination. Get yourself an accountability or goal buddy who'll ensure you'll get stuff done. You can find someone with goals similar to yours so you both can be each other's accountability buddies. It can be a friend, co-worker, boss, life coach or anyone else who influences you positively and can be trusted. The key is they should be able to help you stay on the productivity track each time you digress from your goals or slip into procrastination. You are less likely to go back on your word if you are accountable for your actions.

In this accountability or goal buddy relationship, you connect with the person at regular intervals to update him or her about your progress. For example, let's say your goal is to create an antique selling business because there's a lot of money to be made there.

Think about everything you need to accomplish your bigger goal. You must find out where you can source these antique form – maybe a list of antique dealers within and outside the country. You will also need extensive knowledge of art and history to grade and categorize these antiques for their correct worth. You will need to find a warehouse to store them and a shop front for retailing them. Then, you'll need to get the word out there with slick marketing and promotion techniques. Again, you'll need someone to look after accounts, finances, and invoices.

Thus, at every stage of setting up your antique business, you are accountable for your actions to your buddy. How far have you reached the knowledge acquisition stage? Have you built a list of dealers whom you can source from? Have you read up on laws related to importing and exporting antiques? Have you worked out a revenue model for the business? Are you marketing and promotional activities in place? What about administration, accounts, and finances?

You keep your buddy frequently updated about your progress through the goal fulfillment process. This keeps you on track because you don't want to be viewed as someone who doesn't fulfill a commitment or worse, be admonished by your buddy for inaction!

Optimize your environment to kill procrastination

How do you plan to get anything done is your phone beeps at unimaginable decibels levels each time someone texts you (or there's some activity on your social media feed) or someone is playing a virtual game at a deafening sound alongside you?

Much of our productivity and procrastination is driven by our environment. Beware of technology that can sap your "doing mode" and plunge into "passive viewing mode." Tons of applications and social media channels have been designed to help you believe that you are getting things done when you are plainly wasting time. Emails, messengers, social media feeds, "aimless internet research" are all culprits that can lead you into procrastination.

When you are preoccupied with something important, turn off all notifications on unwanted applications! Do not get on the internet until you've completed the current task.

Don't turn it into a guilt loop

The most unfortunate thing about procrastination is that it creates an unfortunate circle or loop of guilt and regret, leading to even more procrastination. Once you realize that you've been procrastinating, forgive yourself and get your act together. Stop killing yourself about the past.

Avoid thinking, "I should've tackled this earlier" or "I am always procrastinating" or "I don't manage to get anything done since I am a big loser." This makes things worse. Research has proven forgiving you for past procrastination prevents you from putting off tasks for later. Your sense of accountability will increase, and you'll end up getting more done.

If you are overcome by the guilt and regret of doing much in the past, you'll stay in that space. However, if you forgive yourself and let yourself know that there's still time to get your act together, you have a good chance of channelizing your efforts productively.

I'd go a step ahead and say use past procrastination to your benefit. How can that be done? Well, identify what made you avoid productive tasks. Fear, exhaustion, stress, lack of direction, zero accountability? Address these challenges in the future. For example, if you realize that lack of accountability was the primary reason why we're unable to get stuff done, get an accountability buddy or build an accountability blog. If it is fear of failure that led you into procrastination, what are the steps you'll take to experience lesser fear and feel more empowered the next time? You can post your goals on social media, and share your milestones/progress as and when you accomplish them.

Identifying the cause of past failure is the key to taking action to avoid procrastination in the future. Watch out for your negative self-talk. Avoid using terms and phrases such as "need to," "must do" or "have to." These suggest that you don't have a choice, and ends up making you feel more disempowered. Instead try saying, "I choose." It will change how you feel about the task. You'll feel more empowered and in control of the workload.

Get Out of the Excuse Mindset

Excuses kill your mojo. Yep, they destroy your spirit slowly but surely. They stop you in your track and prevent you from taking any further action in the direction of your goals. Going after what you truly desire can be a daunting task. Your mind can create plenty of excuses for why your dreams are far-fetched and not a great idea.

You may have several reasons to not do something up your sleeve currently. Excuses are wonderful at trying to persuade you into inaction. They'll also give you a bunch of reasons why you can't create what you desire in life. They may stretch as far as telling you that your dreams aren't designed for reality. Let us just say, its bullshit! If you can dream of accomplishing something, you can do it.

Stop treating your fears like it's the truth. Use them as tools that drive your energy and enthusiasm. Use them as inspiration to guide you into action. If you operate with an excuse mindset, it's time to switch the channel! Yes, from FearX to EmpowerX). The more you align yourself with what excites you, the more you empower yourself to build a life of your dreams. Switch your energy from excuse mode to action mode now.

I want you to write down your biggest and most common excuse in life? These are the words you use when you have a conversation with yourself or even speak aloud. My number one excuse at one point was, "I don't have time." When it came to accomplishing my goals and dreams, I'd always reinforce the lack of time in working towards my dream life. Identify your excuse and write it on a piece of paper. Ask yourself what enthusiasm will brew inside you and come to the fore if weren't overcome by fear. Clue: the enthusiasm is lying beneath the fear.

Then convert that excitement and enthusiasm into an empowering statement. It's a multi-step process that can convert your excuses into an empowerment filled mindset.

Let us consider an example. You want to launch a start-up in an emerging and field and make neat profits. Identify the excuse that is preventing you from launching your dream start-up. "I think I'll fail and the idea won't work out." Now take a deep breath and feel this fear, uncertainty insecurity within your body, and elsewhere.

Ask yourself, "What excitement is being hidden from the surface by this fear?" The possibility of starting something big, doing what you love, and making money from it excites you.

Your empowering statement is, "I am genuinely building my passion and making money through what I love doing."

See it? Now you are talking! Note the difference. Can you feel the change in the way you've replaced the excuse with joy, passion, and excitement inside? There are tons of possibilities brewing within you now. This inspiration becomes the primary source of action.

Now use this new-found inspiration and enthusiasm as support and come up with a statement that affirms your positive energy each time you find yourself lying in a pit of excuses. Remind your excuses that you are transforming, and you are not feeding them anymore. Instead, you are focusing your energy towards enthusiasm and action. Over a period of time, you'll find these excuses fading into oblivion. Trust the fact that you are complete within yourself to accomplish exactly what you want to accomplish or fulfill your dreams.

The Five-Minute Magic

This is one of the most effective strategies for people struggling with procrastination. The Five-Minute Miracle is about questioning yourself along the line of "What action can I take in under five minutes today that takes this task even a tiny bit ahead? Once you nailed that one small action, set your timer for five minutes. Spend the next five minutes exclusively on the task. According to research, once you just begin something, you are more likely to do it. Instead of simply contemplating doing something, start with the tiniest bit action.

This psychological principle is referred to as the Zeigarnik effect. It says that unfinished tasks are likelier to get stuck in a loop in our memory. This is exactly things we didn't do play in a loop in our thoughts. Even the smallest action is action after all. Five minutes make a world of difference!

Try the power hour technique. A power hour comprises putting away all distractions and working single-mindedly on a task. Start by keeping aside all distractions and putting in concentrated blocks of time (start with 20-minute blocks). This is followed by brief periods of rest for leveraging uninterrupted time to optimize brain and body foundation.

Research has proven that the human brain naturally moves through peaks and indent cycles. To optimize our productivity, it is important that you respect the peaks and indents by balancing focused, dedicated time with integrated, leisure and relaxation.

Select your own procrastination song

Pick a song of your choice that makes you feel energized, inspired and charged to go out there and conquer the world. Play it each time you have to deal with a task that you've been procrastinating on. The brain has a trigger for creating new habits. Each time you play the song and get stuff done, your brain associates the song with "doing." You are likelier to follow through when you feel wonderful in your body and mind.

Create the task you've been outing off as a rough draft

Let us say you want to create an authority blog about weight loss for women populated with several information-rich blog posts, reviews and stories but find the process of creating this blog from scratch highly overwhelming and intimidating.

The key is to prepare a rough draft, which is comparatively less stressful, tiresome and overwhelming. You start by brainstorming ideas about what you want to include in the blog. Key blog topics, personal stories of readers, weight loss supplement reviews, a forum where women looking to lose weight can support, inspire and guide each other and so on.

Creating a rough draft will free up plenty of hesitation, uncertainty, and pressure about completing the entire task. Each time I am overcome by procrastination, I get down to scribbling key ideas to get started without the burden of doing something big. Tell yourself that it is only a rough draft.

Psychologically, you are tricking your brain into thinking that it isn't real. If our brain believes the task is not for real, it won't experience the same pressure as it does during crucial tasks. The next day, start off where you left with the rough draft gradually. Start with 1-2 blog posts a day. Finalize it, edit it, rework on it (or any similar action) before sending or publishing it. Wham, you just did something you believed you couldn't. Now you have a weight loss blog with a couple of blog posts. Not bad!

Next, tackle the next two blog posts based on your rough draft, polish it and publish it. There, now you four information-rich blog posts. Keep going back to your rough draft for inspiration. Once you create a mock or rough version, you are likelier to complete a goal to its fruition.

Don't wait until you are in the mood

When it comes to getting stuff done, we keep telling ourselves we are not in the mood. It happens to the best of us. We wait until we feel we are in the "mood" to do something. You don't have to be in the mood to take action. For example, if you want to be an author, you have to set a time and goal for writing each day, irrespective of whether you age in the mood or not. You pick a time to sit and write a designated number of pages each day. That's how it works when you have to get stuff done!

You can't be pumped up and inspired all the time, even if you are in a creative profession. At times, you just have to go out there and get the job done whether you are in the mood or not. You have to consistent action in that direction of your goals no matter whether you feel like doing something or not.

Keep asking yourself about what needs to be done next. You don't have to delay beginning until you have an impeccable or elaborate plan before you even start. Center yourself and ask what exactly you want, what is currently right for you and what can take you forward in life. Keep moving ahead even if it is by half an inch.

David Bailey
Chapter Four:

Time Management Secrets

A university professor has three different bags of sand, pebbles and huge rocks each along with a bucket. He requests a volunteer to empty all three stone grades in the bucket. A student steps up to carry the task meticulously. He starts with the sand, followed by pebbles and rocks, unable to fit everything it all in the bucket.

The professor then turns to the class and says, if only he's put in the rocks first, followed by pebbles and sand, everything would've fit in. Time management is pretty much the same – organizing your pebbles, sand, and rocks to fit it all in. Focus on completing your biggest tasks first to leave room for mid-sized and small ones. When you focus on the smaller tasks first, there is a tendency to spend more time on them than needed leaving little time for performing medium and big tasks efficiently.

Time management is all about planning and organizing your time to accomplish optimal productivity. If you don't plan time slots for large tasks or rocks, the sand and pebbles (or small and medium-sized tasks) will take your time.

Time is wealth. Everyone has 24 hours in a day, yet successful and wealthy people are able to leverage the power of their 24 hours to do much more than people who complain they "never have enough time" to do anything. It is the same tool. However, the way it is utilized makes all the difference.

How do some people always manage to complete their tasks and even find time for leisure activities while others struggle to meet deadlines? How are some people always ahead of their schedule while others grapple with things at the last minute? It is all a game of slick time management. How you utilize the 24 hours at your disposal to pack in as much productivity as you can make all the difference.

Here are some of the best time management hacks that can skyrocket you from procrastination to productivity.

Prioritize tasks based on four quadrants

Okay, so you have 20 different tasks to do but don't know which one, to begin with or finish first. Prioritization of tasks is the key. This is a simple yet highly effective method when it comes to prioritizing tasks. Doing this before going to bed each day or the beginning of a day will help simplify and clarify your schedule for the day.

Make four quadrants in your notepad – 1. urgent and important 2. Important but not urgent 3. Urgent but not important and 4. Not important and not urgent. Next, categorize every task based on each of these four quadrants.

Let's say you have a client presentation coming up in the next couple of days. It's an important account, and you can bag a huge contract from the client if done right. So, working on the presentation is important and urgent. These tasks should be your first priority since they are both time-bound and crucial. Don't put them off for later. Tackle them as soon as possible.

Next, come tasks that are important yet not urgent. A client may ask you to submit a rough draft before beginning a project. It may not be a time-bound task, but it's still important and needs to be completed before you begin working on the project. This makes this an important and not urgent task, which should be next to your priority list after tasks that are both urgent and important.

Now, a restaurant whose hospitality you enjoyed last night may ask you to fill a feedback form and return it until tomorrow for filing their records. The task seems urgent because its time-bound but is it really important for you? No really. These are tasks that are urgent but not important and should be third of your priority list.

The urgent yet not important can be delegated to someone else as they are urgent though not important. It doesn't matter if you don't do them yourself. Spend time and energy on completing tasks that are urgent and important, while delegating the not important yet urgent tasks to someone else. This is how smart and successful people leverage their time. They spend their time and energy on high priority and important tasks. Leverage the time and effort of other people to get more done.

Finally, tasks that are neither urgent nor important can wait until you complete tasks from the other three quadrants. For example, completing the next two levels of a virtual game your friend has challenged you to is neither urgent not important. It can wait until you've completed the more urgent and important tasks.

Make it a habit of doing this every day. At the end of the day, go over the entire day's activities to tally every task against the four quadrants. In the end, note which quadrant tasks you've spent maximum time completing. If you are spending time on the tasks that are not important (third quadrant) or that are neither important nor urgent (fourth quadrant), you need to get your act in place.

Start each day by creating a list of 2-3 tasks that are both important and urgent (first quadrant) before moving on to other categories. As you finish each task, tick it on the list to award yourself a sense of fulfillment and accomplishment, which can inspire you to do even more.

We have plenty of downtime throughout the day. Use this downtime productively to make your task priority list. How about using your commuting time (if you aren't driving obviously) for planning and organizing the day's activities? Ensure that you don't devote all your free time to planning, which can turn counterproductive by wearing you out. Let's say you have about 10-15 minutes of downtime, use the first couple of minutes for planning and getting organized.

I'd even recommend utilizing a wee bit of your weekends. There is a meme doing the rounds on the internet about a man tossing papers in the air and saying something to the effect, "*#*% you, its Friday." The next image then has Monday written on it, and the same man is picking up all the papers he'd thrown on Friday. Doing even little work during the weekend can eliminate considerable pressure from your work week. Even if it's something as simple as creating a rough draft or planning your week ahead! Spend 2-4 hours each day being productive. You'll still be left with plenty of time for relaxation, leisure activities and spending time with your loved ones. Try squeezing in tasks into your downtime and weekends, and note the difference it makes to your overall productivity.

I know some super successful people who plan their entire week on a Sunday. This helps them focus on their priorities and smoothly transition into the next week. Once you slip into a relaxed weekend mindset, it's tough to suddenly make your way into a productive Monday mindset. By putting the place in place on Sunday, you make the transition less stressful.

How to Turn Procrastination into Productivity
Eliminate time wasters and bad habits

I'll suggest a quick exercise to help you identify where a majority of your time is invested. Do the seven-day audit. What are you doing currently? Record it in a phone app or journal. You can break it 30- or 60-minute blocks. Did you get a lot done? Was its time effectively spent? Did you waste time? If you are using the above mentioned four-quadrant method, categorize everything you do base on the four quadrants. At the end of the week, tally all numbers. Where was a majority of your time spent? Which quadrant did you most occupy? The insights may surprise you!

Bad habits are one of the biggest time wasters designed purely to kill productivity. The most unfortunate thing is these time wasters come attached with the illusion that we are getting a lot done. For instance, you may aimlessly browse the internet under the notion of doing research or looking for ideas. Is it adding real value to your overall task?

Binge-watching Netflix, surfing social media incessantly, playing virtual games, going for drinks with friends frequently are all negative habits that take away from the valuable little time resources we have. Utilize your time judiciously if you are keen on accomplishing your goals. The big difference between winners and losers is if the former manages to delay gratification and focus on the task at hand while keeping their vision on the bigger picture. They are keener on long-term rewards, which pushes them in the direction of their goals through productive utilization of time.

All of us envy the rich, successful and famous yet we aren't prepared to go through the struggle they go through and the things they give up to reach a certain position or level of success in life. There is plenty of hard work, sacrifice, delayed gratification, and blood/sweat behind the success. And then you wonder why you aren't as successful as the people you admire. Are you prepared to give up your bad habits and delay gratification like them? Are you prepared to be productive and hustle every day like them? Do you have it in you to delay short-term gratification in exchange for long-term rewards? Use your time wisely if you are serious about becoming successful and wealthy.

You aren't accomplishing anything by watching Netflix (other than making Netflix richer) unless you are a scriptwriter or movie maker fishing for ideas. Channelize every minute towards productivity. If tasks get too overwhelming, take a break.

Have you read Charles Duhig's book titled *The Power of Habit?* In the book, he describes keystone habits that hold all our other stones. These keystone habits don't just help draw other good habits but also help a person get rid of bad or unproductive habits. By focusing on keystone habits, you learn to manage your overall time effective, which makes the process of habit development easier.

All the same, it is important to train and nurture the other side of your brain. Spend time pursuing things that are outside your comfort zone. If you are a medical practitioner, go out there and learn to dance. A violin player can learn kickboxing or taekwondo. Go beyond your predictable comfort zone to explore newer hobbies and pursuits to boost your chances of success. You end up expanding your brain's capacity, while also acquiring new skills in the bargain.

Set Periodic Reminders

Set alarms on your phone or other devices or create visual reminders of tasks that are to be completed. Set a reminder for the final deadline. However, also set reminders for sub-deadlines for staying on track throughout the process. For example, let us say you have a project that is due in the next 3 weeks, you may want to set reminders not just at the end of 21 days but also day 7, 10, 15 and 17. This ensures you don't scurry around like a headless bird on the final day of your deadline to get the task done. You are reminded of the task throughout it, which is likelier to keep you on schedule.

Avoid multitasking

Do not live under the illusion that if you are doing two things together, you are getting more done. In fact, you are taking longer to finish both the tasks than you would have if you'd tackle them individually. Avoid trying to be "superhuman" and instead focus on being efficient. When you take on too many things at a time, you can give concentrated focus, attention, and energy to any one task. You are likelier to be more efficient by devoting all your time and energy to one task before taking on another.

For example, let's say instead of answering emails and making phone calls at one time (which is switching your brain back and forth and making you ineffectual in the process), if you simply reply to all the emails first and then start returning the calls, you'll perform both the tasks with increased efficiency.

Group all similar tasks together, and create a schedule to handle them at one time instead of squeezing them in frequently with other tasks. For instance, instead of responding to every email that pops into your box throughout the day, schedule a time to tackle all emails together at the end of the day or start of the next day. This way you won't be frequently distracted from other tasks throughout the day, and can also respond to your emails in a focused and attentive manner.

Similarly, if you friendly meet people who pitch their services to you (vendors, professionals, etc.), reserve a specific day or days to meet them instead of having them walk in and out of your office throughout the week. This way you can work undisturbed on other tasks for the rest of your work week. The idea is to group similar tasks together and schedule them at one time, so you don't go back and forth from one task to another and build the momentum required to complete a single task in a focused, efficient manner. Don't slow your brain down by taking on too many things at a time.

Understand the importance of delegating responsibility. The Pareto Principle says 80 percent of our results come from 20 percent of our efforts. Identify what 20 percent of your efforts are creating the 80 percent results and spend more time in those pursuits. Similarly, be smart and delegate tasks that are consuming a major chunk of your time but not adding considerably to the results. For example, if you observe that a major portion of your time is invested in sending emails and paying out invoices, hire someone to do the task for you while focusing more on tasks that are bringing you results.

In their bid to get a lot done, people end up over-scheduling. At times, we are tempted to take on more than we can handle, but that's not always a good idea. Try to be practical, realistic and easy on yourself by scheduling tasks that you are confident of accomplishing in the given time.

Don't always attempt to take extra work or overschedule to impress or help other people.

For instance, if your manager or co-worker says they need something done at the end of the day, and you are already neck deep in work, say something like, "I am slightly overloaded with work today, but I sure can hand it to you by noon tomorrow." You are being honest about your time limitations without saying a no. Don't push yourself to do more than what you can handle.

Master the ability to say no if you have other important things to do. It doesn't make you a bad person. Respect your time, and teach people to value it too. Over scheduling leads to increased stress, and reduced productivity.

Also, avoid rushing from one task to another. It'll end up stifling your productivity and efficiency. You'll find it challenging to stay focused, inspired and motivated is you move from task to task at breakneck speed. Instead, allow yourself some downtime between tasks. Breathe. Take in some fresh air, allows your brains to oxygenate, go for a walk, listen to music, paint, meditate or other mind cleansing exercise.

Working for extended spells kills our motivation, energy, and focus. After working for a few hours (1-3 hours) our brain starts slacking off, and we get invariably distracted. This is when all the daydreaming, doodling and social media surfing happens. The brain is exhausted and seeks some relief in the form of more instant pleasure or gratification giving activities that distract it from the overwhelming stress and exhaustion.

Use this solution each time the procrastination monster comes baying for your blood. As soon as you find yourself slacking, take a break immediately and do a mind-clearing exercise.

Mind clearing exercise can be any activity that needs focus and attentiveness. The objective is to do exactly what the name implies – clear our mind from the accumulated cobwebs. De-cluttering the mind is important if you want to approach the next task with efficiency. After working on a task for long, your brain is brimming with information. It is filled with upcoming tasks, information from previous tasks and plenty of other hoopla. Of course, it needs to recuperate.

Activities that shift your focus give your brain much needed rest, which is why you can return to the task feeling recharged, refreshed and rejuvenated. You are all fired up to tackle the new task!

Let's look at some mind-clearing exercises that are simple yet effective when it comes to increasing focus when you are working for longer time spells.

Meditation. The objective of meditation is to quieten the mind, calm your spirit and help you achieve a deeper connection with yourself. Sit still and mindfully focus on your breathing and physical sensations. At times, imagine yourself in a serene, quiet and positive setting. You can imagine being in a place that you find positively relaxing and energizing, like your favorite vacation destination, a lush garden, flourishing mountains or a tropical island/beach.

Hard exercise. Launch into intense cardio, push-ups, weights or sit-ups.

Go for a leisurely walk. Enjoy a leisurely walk in the neighborhood, focusing on mindful walking, while also taking in the natural beauty of your surroundings.

Listening to music is therapeutic, and increases the secretion of our brain's feel-good hormones. Find the perfect tune for your mood or listen to a haunting, soulful piano rendition. Music is an instant mood changer. It is known to boost your physical, emotional and spiritual state. Try to play music that makes you feel positive, lively and upbeat.

Sauna release. Enjoy sweating in intense heat as sweating also activates our feel-good hormones, and makes us feel positive and rejuvenated. Accompany the practice of sauna with meditation, music or reading.

Pet therapy. You are lucky if you have a pet. Spending time with your pets is believed to be extremely therapeutic. Allow yourself some time off with these adorable little creatures that rejuvenate your senses. Sweep into their world of unconditional love and buddy experiences. Some of the simplest things in life give big pleasures and help us experience true happiness.

Reading. Make time for slow reading purely for entertainment or pleasure. Let words and ideas surround you and whisk you into another world for a while.

Power naps. Power naps work wonderfully well for me. When you are working for a long time, and your body feels like its drifting away, don't fight or resist it. Instead, listen to it and enjoy a short, power nap. Even a 7-15 nap is enough to recharge your senses and rejuvenate your spirit. The brain gets its much-needed rest, and you are raring to go with another task.

It isn't always possible to move away from work or squeeze in even a small mind clearing exercise. In such a scenario, it is best to take a bathroom water break or stretch/meditate for a couple of minutes. All your brain needs are a couple of minutes!

Chapter Five:

Be the Ultimate Self-Discipline Ninja

"Read 500 pages like this every day. That's how knowledge works. It builds up, like compound interest. All of you can do it, but I guarantee not many of you will do it." — Warren Buffett

Be an early riser

The early hours of your day are a time for quiet contemplation and relaxation, where you remain undisturbed for a while at the start of the day. Some of the world's most successful people are known to be "the 5 a.m. people."

They rise early and spend time in the wee hours of the morning reflecting about their day and goals. This is also the best time to do your meditation and guided visualization. Even if you aren't a morning person, make incremental changes in your everyday routine. Start by waking 15 minutes earlier than your usual time for the first week. Make it 30 minutes the week after that and so on until you are able to raise a couple of hours earlier than usual.

A majority of the world's most successful people begin their day early and tackle their toughest tasks during the early part of the day to smoothly set themselves up for the rest of their day. They don't begin their day at 12 pm. One of the best ways to make the most of your day is to attack your day with gusto. There are tons of advantages of being an early riser.

Say Cheese

Research has consistently confirmed that people with authentic smiles, also known as Duchenne smiles, are much happier and fulfilled. This is one of the most effective habits to maintain your mental, psychological and spiritual peace over a period of time. The body's physiology dictates our mind's psychology and vice versa. When we sit in a slouched position or frown, it signals depression and despair. Our mind quickly picks up these clues and begins to experience similar feelings.

However, once you make a change in the outward appearance or assume more confident, happy power positions, the mind quickly responds to this, thus adjusting your inner feelings. Make a change outside to impact how you feel from within.

Eat Breakfast

Breakfast is indeed the most important meal of your day, yet shockingly 31 million Americans skip it every day. Can you imagine? If you are dead serious about becoming successful, consume a healthy and nutrition filled breakfast each morning. It doesn't take much effort, only some planning. If you are running to work each morning with little or no time for breakfast, rise early and make time for this habit right away. It impacts your entire day, energy and productivity.

Another super habit that has astronomical healthy benefits is drinking a tall glass of lemon water daily. Lemons are an important Vitamin C source, while also possessing multiple health benefits. They aid with digestion, boost the immune, cleanse the body from toxins and rehydrate it, all of which is important if you want to stay energetic and productive throughout the day.

The water helps eliminate toxins from the system each morning. Over a period of time, this habit helps with weight reduction, lower inflammations, and an overall energy boost. And we all know we can do that extra energy zing when it comes to accomplishing our tasks and goals.

Apart from a healthy breakfast, focus on consuming healthy meals throughout the day. Nothing will dampen your mind, mind spirit (and in turn ability to function effectively) than an imbalanced and low nutrition meal. Ensure you eat well, and at regular intervals to keep your body sufficiently nourished.

Portion your meals to eat about three to four large or five to six mid-sized meals if you are also exercising or practicing some form of physical fitness. Consume smaller, healthier snacks or meals throughout the day. Include nuts, fruits, raw vegetables and natural, homemade dips like hummus. Avoid eating greasy, high fat, artificially flavored and saccharine laden food. Canned, processed and preservative filled food also makes you feel low on energy while adding zero nutritional value to your body.

To prevent hunger pangs from ruining your focus, eat healthy snack fillers such as energy bars, fruits, fresh fruit juices and smoothies, yogurt, raw veggie sticks and so on. As far as possible, eat at the same time every day instead of varying your meal timings.

Make a meal plan to consume more nutrition laden foods. This should be like a blueprint of your meals for the week. Roughly calculate the amount of nutrition your body gets with each meal. A meal plan will help you make smarter food dietary choices.

Consume more lean protein as part of your diet. Lean proteins are low fat and high nutrition based. Select foods like eggs, legumes, and poultry, while avoiding fatty proteins such as processed meat and bacon. Again, whole grain-based foods such as whole wheat pasta, brown rice, and whole wheat bread makes for healthier food choices. Switch from flour-based foods to whole grain foods. They are high in protein, fiber, and other nutrients. Ditch white pasta and bread and op for oats, millet, and barley instead.

Eat more mindfully and intentionally. Avoid emotion driven binge-eating. Let your emotions not dictate your food choices. Do not grab your lunch while working furiously on your system. Take a few minutes off from work to eat more mindfully. Be aware of the impact of the food on your senses, while appreciate its taste, aroma, and texture. Observe experience and chew every morsel carefully. Mindless and psychologically driven eating is one of the biggest causes for eating disorders.

Keep your body sufficiently hydrated throughout the day. Drink a minimum of 8 large glasses water each day. Minimize intake of caffeine, alcohol and sweetened beverages. You are what you eat. When you make smarter and healthier eating choices, you are setting yourself up for a healthy mind and body in the long run, which is integral to the process of working hard and accomplishing your goals. If your body is fit and healthy, you aren't going to get much done.

Exercise

One of the very best habits you can inculcate in life is to exercise or practice some form of physical fitness activity each day, irrespective of how busy or preoccupied you are. Exercise doesn't always mean running in marathons, doing intense cardio or weightlifting. Even lightly strenuously physical fitness activities are known to increase oxygen supply to our blood. Plus, exercise boosts the secretion of endorphins or feel-good hormones in our brain, which leaves us feeling positive.

If you aren't an exercise person, replace more strenuous tasks with more fun and interesting activities such as dancing, Zumba, aerobics, cycling, swimming, skating, aerobics and more. Combining exercise and leisure will help you have fun while giving your body its fitness dose.

Exercising daily will not just make you feel better physically but also help increase your motivation, focus, mental clarity, and emotional well-being, all of which are integral to the process of goal fulfillment. Regular exercise increases the body's dopamine level, and releases more serotonin into the system, giving us an almost euphoric feeling without using drugs.

Make it a habit to walk 10,000 steps a day. Most people fall terribly short of this goal on a daily basis. On an average, Americans walk 5,117 steps a day. This is one power-packed habit if you do more sedentary work. Park your vehicle slightly further from the workplace and take the stairs instead of elevator to increase your daily steps count.

Take a walk for 10-15 minutes each morning before beginning your day. Fresh air, nature, and exercise is a wonderful combination that can do a world of good to your body, mind and spirit.

Take more vitamins and minerals

Americans don't get the required mineral and vitamin intake according to several nutrition researches. It's more processed food, carb, refined sugar, and other unhealthy food based. Find vitamin and mineral supplements that can be consumed daily to make up for any deficiency. The consequence of ignoring your body's needs may not be immediate.

However, over a longer period of time, it can be damaging. This impacts us over a longer period of time where physical, mental, emotional and spiritual clarity is concerned.

Invest in Yourself

It is often challenging to stay motivated over a long period of time. Remember, your biggest investment is going to be yourself. Wealthy and successful people always realize that there is no greater investment than themselves! They'll seize every opportunity to upgrade their skills, find lucrative investment opportunities, enhance their learning, and spend precious time engaging in constructive, self-improvement activities. Their focus will be on investing in skills, knowledge and other attributes that add value to their ultimate goal.

You can tell much about a person's character and personality by observing how they invest their spare hours.

Actively work on your bucket list instead of flowing with the tide. As a person destined and gearing for success, you must have a bucket list of your goals, plans, and aspirations. It is like a life map that lays out all that you want to go ahead. Keep adding new items to your bucket list. I'd recommend starting with a list of 50 things that you most want to do accomplish in your life. Keep working on fulfilling one item on your bucket list before moving to the next. Add new goals to keep you inspired, excited and stimulated. You want to live and conquer not just exist and survive! There's a huge difference.

Another amazing thing you can do for yourself is invest in a life coach or mentor. A coach helps channelize your efforts and offers you a well-laid out, actionable plan to chase them. They may help you become the best version of yourself by helping you unlock your true potential. Rich and successful people view their coach as their success partners.

Each of us has plenty of unused, dormant potential lying inside us, which needs to be leveraged to the fullest. A qualified, professional and experienced coach can help you tap into your innermost potential to accomplish a dream life.

By investing in yourself, you'll embrace plenty of opportunities. Do you really believe anyone will be willing to invest in your business or you if you aren't sure of yourself? Confidence and self-assurance come to investing in ourselves physically, mentally, emotionally and spiritually on a daily basis. You transform into the most superior version of yourself, which in turn helps you attract opportunities and people like magnets.

It is not easy to stay motivated for a long span of time, especially when you don't witness tangible results. We often get discouraged and disappointed by our goals and are tempted maneuver off the track. Inspire yourself each day to accomplish more.

Read inspiring and information-rich blogs, follow the blog of people you admire, seek inspiration from the challenges and stories of other people who have fulfilled their dreams. Do all this during your power hour (the magical early morning time when there's more peace and less distraction to contend with). Watch motivational videos on YouTube, listen to audio books while going about your daily morning routine, listen to inspiring podcasts of people who've been there and done that. Quality input always leads to quality output. What you feed your mind and spirit is determined by your actions, which are directly responsible for your success. This is similar to feed healthy and nutritious food to your body. You ate nourishing your mind and spirit.

Success people barely expend their time on futile pursuits. According to a research, only 9 percent of wealthy people watch reality shows, compared to 78 percent of poor. While the non-performers are busy watching television, the wealthy are hustling their way into even more wealth and success. And then we complain about the disparity in income.

The cold, hard fact is the wealthy are chasing their goals with gusto. They spend time reading books about finances and investment. They almost always make optimal utilization of their time to create, reinvent and find ways to be more effective at their job or business. You'll spot them voraciously consuming books about investment, money, business, social skills, communication skills, psychology, market dynamics, self-development – whatever boosts their knowledge to give them an edge over others.

If you want to rich, powerful, successful and productive, possess an insatiable curiosity to understand how things can be more effective. Then apply this knowledge to make yourself more resourceful and marketable. Even when the wealthy accomplish their financial goals, they don't stop learning. It is a life-long process to learn, acquire new skills, grow, build new things/businesses, and flourish. This, while others are busy binge-watching Netflix or spending hours on their gaming console!

Attend seminars, conferences, workshops and other business networking events where you can listen to and meet people you admire. This gives you added inspiration and zing to stay motivated while running after your goals. This is the nourishment your mind and soul need from time to time. The rich a successful will never give up an opportunity to upgrade their knowledge and skills. They strive to mingle with like-minded people and learn from them. Inspiration is the gateway to accomplishing glory because anything the mind can perceive, we can create. Stay focused, inspired and motivated by investing in yourself periodically.

Networking is integral to the process of investing in yourself. Build a contact list of influential and inspiring people.

One of the signature attributes of the rich and successful is that they are focused on ideas. This includes meditation, tapping into their intuition, conversing with other rich and successful people, reading inspiring blogs, eliminating toxic people from their life, taking classes, pursuing creative activities such as art, learning new languages, taking up hobbies and more. They show an inclination for ideas, for pursuits that enhance their creativity, capacity to generate ideas and productivity. You'll often find some of the most inspiring people talking about ideas rather than challenges. They'll be talking more about solution and ideas than cribbing about challenging situations. Plug into these conversations at networking events to notice how it's all about ideas and visions for the successful.

Another important aspect about investing in yourself is trusting and respecting your intuition. Develop a keen connection with your inner self through practices such as meditation, mindful breathing, yoga, and visualization. It will help you tap effectively into your inner faculties, which is important for the idea generation and decision-making process. Honor your inner voice and gut feeling. It will offer you greater focus, mindfulness, and clarity while making important decisions.

Make your intuition rock solid, and avoid letting other people's feelings, ideas, beliefs, and thoughts determine the direction of your life. It is highly empowering and liberating to lean on your intuition for making faster, better and smarter decisions. In a majority of the times I haven't pay heed to my intuition, I've ended up making a regretful decision. Build, nurture, and learn to have faith in your intuition.

Increase your personal value

Think you are a product. Yes, that is tip number one when it comes to increasing your personal brand value. You are a brand with your own distinguishable features and benefits – all waiting to be upgraded one year after another. Differentiate yourself from others by creating your own, unique personal brand. Companies spend a large amount of time listening to their customer needs while improving their products and services. They do this to increase their sales and overall all efficiency. You can also undertake continuous product improvement on yourself to increase your overall value as an entrepreneur or employee and differentiate yourself from other entrepreneurs or employees.

You are work in progress. The day you stop learning, growing and upgrading, your downfall begins. Self-improvement doesn't have to be pricey. My favorite knowledge up gradation tip is to pick one topic a year. For instance, let us say I want to learn everything I can about Facebook advertising. I'll go to the library or Kindle every month and issue or download a different title about Facebook advertising for an entire year. Can you imagine the knowledge you'll gain by reading books about a single topic for an entire year?

Pick any topic that you want to gain more knowledge or information about. It can be anything from baking to travel photography to project management to conversation skills. Think about how many topics or subjects you'll end up becoming an expert in within the next 5-10 years. These tiny yet winsome habits make all the difference in your life and career.

Another top line habit of the rich and successful is that they boost to enhance their learning curve through speed reading and learning. Start your day by reading books that are currently relevant to you. They may offer insights into challenges and issues going on in your life currently. Speed reading is believed to be a habit of several successful folks, including George Washington and Abraham Lincoln. It helps for long-term success!

I was interviewing candidates to fill a job position. Predictably, they ran me through what they've accomplished in the last few years to become better versions of themselves. On asking one candidate what he'd done to enhance his skills, efficiency in the last few years, he said, "nothing really, I graduated from university last year, and now I am finally done with my education" Goes without saying, he didn't get the job.

Most successful people realize that learning is a continuous and lifelong pursuit. There are tons of inspiring stories about people who get back to college and embarking on a completely different career path after raising children. Take the stories of people who've been laid off owing to downsizing. They go on to obtain training, education, and certifications to completely successfully switch careers. The foundation for all your accomplishments is the willingness, flexibility, and openness to absorbing new knowledge. This is how to increase your personal brand value from time to time.

The more you learn, the more you'll realize how little you know. The best and fastest way to enhance your worth as an entrepreneur or employee is to keep learning and growing. Treat yourself as a competitive market product which has to work upon itself year after year to increase its overall worth. Instead of wishing for everything to be easier, wish that you become better! And the only way to become better is through constant learning.

Spend 15-30 minutes on focused thinking daily

Building wealth and success takes years of self-discipline, smart financial decisions, and perseverance. Tom Corley, a financial planner, spent half a decade interviewing more than 200 wealthy people, a majority of them being self-made millionaires. Their daily habits among other things included spending 15-30 minutes on minutes on focused thinking.

In his bestseller, *Change Your Habits, Change Your Life,* Corey talks about how the rich and successful people manufacture their destiny and good fortune through carefully cultivated lifestyle habits. Several self-made millionaires interviewed by Corley said they take time out to process and reflect upon things currently happening in their lives.

They take time out to think to reflect and contemplate in isolation for at least 15 minutes each morning. They tend to reflect on their health, personal relationships, and professional acquisitions. Having quiet, contemplative moments are integral to the process of stress reduction. Even something as simple as devoting a couple of minutes for focused breathing helps eliminate stress.

Convert challenges into opportunities

We are all tempted to think that successful and rich people are those who've had smooth sailing and never experienced setbacks or failures in life. Au contraire, they have several challenges and setbacks which they cleverly convert into opportunities. That is the difference between the average and a wealthy mindset. They use failures as stepping stones to success and convert obstacles and challenges into learning and opportunities.

One of my closest friends was laid off from the job after his company began downsizing due to curb rising operational costs. Predictably, he was depressed and stressed about how he would support his family, while also paying his mortgage and bills. After drowning in self-pity for some time, he read something inspiring that changed his perception of the situation. The friend decided to be more proactive, and take control of his life.

He decided to go back to college and finish his education while relying on his savings. He and his partner used all their personal savings to help them tide through the tough phase. His partner took up a few jobs to support the family income, while he focused on getting his degree. The friend also took up part-time jobs during the weekends and evenings to make some money. After getting his degree, the man launched a start-up with an idea he'd been toying with for a while but never had the guts to pursue earlier, comfortable as he was in his cushy, 'secure' 9-5 job, living someone else's dreams and visions instead of fulfilling his own.

He worked hard on his start-up, at times working 20 hours a day. He was barely able to meet the expenditure of running the business initially. However, it picked up gradually. And then, there was no looking back. He began making consistent profits and set a couple of other businesses to become one of the city's most well-known entrepreneurs. Venture capitalists clamored to invest in his ventures.

Do you think all this would've been possible if he hadn't seized a seemingly disastrous situation and converted it into something wonderful? He turned an obstacle into a rewarding opportunity. He would've still been a bucket carrier carrying buckets of water instead of building his own pipeline of wealth. One of the things that set successful people is they possess the vision to convert their challenges into fruitful opportunities.

Think out of the box. Failures and challenges aren't the ends of the road. They can be the beginning of another rewarding path.

In a tiny Italian town, several hundred years ago, there was a small-time trader who owed a sizeable sum of money to a local money lender. The moneylender was an old, evil and unattractive guy who lusted after the trader's daughter. He shrewdly made an offer to the trader that he (the lender) would forgo the trader's debt if the trader let him marry his daughter. The trader was obviously repulsed. The moneylender stated that he would put two pebbles in a bag – one black and another white. The trader's daughter would then have to pick a pebble. If she picked a black pebble, their debt would be erased, and the lender would marry her. However, if it were white, the lender wouldn't marry her, and the loan would still be erased!

The lender then picked up two pebbles from the pebble-strewn path, and while he did so, the daughter noticed that he picked two black pebbles and placed them in the bag. He then urged the daughter to pick one pebble from the bag. Now, she had three options. She could either refused to pick any pebble from the bag, which means her father's debt would not be erased. Take both the pebbles out and expose the cheat money lender. Again, her father's debt would not be erased by doing so. Pick a pebble fully aware that it was a black one and give herself up to erase her father's debt.

She drew out a pebble from the bag and 'accidentally' dropped it among the other pebbles on the path. She looked at the lender and said, "Oh! Please pardon my clumsiness. Never mind though, if you look into your bag for the stone that's left, you'll know exactly which one I picked." There was obviously a black pebble in the bag. Since the money lender didn't want to be seen as a cheat, he remained tight-lipped. He had to pretend that the stone she picked was white, and erase her father's debt while letting her go.

There's a powerful lesson in this story. No matter how tough or challenging a situation, people geared for success will not always limit their thinking to the given options. They train themselves to think out of the box and make the most of their adversity.

David Bailey
Conclusion

Thank you for downloading this book.

I sincerely hope it was able to help you know more about self-discipline, eliminating procrastination and getting into action mode for boosting your overall productivity and chances of success. There are plenty of real, actionable strategies, which you start using immediately. I have included several action plans, practical strategies and proven techniques for increasing your self-discipline muscle, which can help you accomplish your goals.

The book is packed with plenty of time management, resilience building, productivity-boosting, anti-procrastination and other helpful self-discipline hacks that will help you embark you on the productivity path right away.

The next step is to act. A person who does not read is as good as a person who cannot read. Likewise, information without action is futile. You have to get up, go out there, and put self-discipline into practice to make it work for you! You have to sweat it out and give it your all to come out successful. The only metal that goes through the grind becomes gold!

Do what it takes to reach your goals through the right growth mindset, powerful self-discipline strategies, effective goal setting, time management techniques, positive habits, perseverance, and resilience. Remember, the steering wheel of your life is in your hands alone. What you make of your destiny is determined by your words, thoughts, actions, habits, and behavior.

Lastly, if you enjoyed reading the book, please take some time to share your views and post a review. It'd be greatly appreciated.

Here's to a more rewarding, productive, successful and self-discipline filled life!

www.ingramcontent.com/pod-product-compliance
Lightning Source LLC
Chambersburg PA
CBHW020106240426
43661CB00002B/47